William J. Ashley

Edward III & his Wars

1327-1360 - extracts from the chronicles of Froissart, Jehan le Bel, Knighton, Adam of Murimuth, Robert of Avesbury, the Chronicle of Lanercost, the State Papers, and other contemporary records

William J. Ashley

Edward III & his Wars

1327-1360 - extracts from the chronicles of Froissart, Jehan le Bel, Knighton, Adam of Murimuth, Robert of Avesbury, the Chronicle of Lanercost, the State Papers, and other contemporary records

ISBN/EAN: 9783337286347

Printed in Europe, USA, Canada, Australia, Japan

Cover: Foto ©ninafisch / pixelio.de

More available books at **www.hansebooks.com**

ENGLISH HISTORY BY CONTEMPORARY
WRITERS

Edward iij & his Wars
1327—1360

Extracts from the Chronicles of Froissart, Jehan le Bel, Knighton, Adam of Murimuth, Robert of Avesbury, the Chronicle of Lanercost the State Papers, & other contemporary records

ARRANGED AND EDITED BY

W. J. ASHLEY, M.A.

Fellow of Lincoln College, Oxford

LONDON
DAVID NUTT
1887

BEDFORD:
ARTHUR RANSOM, PRINTER, HIGH STREET.

PREFACE.

The age of Edward III. is the age of chivalry. This is alike its praise and its condemnation. Those who care for history because of the bright pictures it brings before them, the moving incident, the gallant feat, will delight in the pages of Froissart and ask no more: while to others the warriors of the 14th century will seem too often mean or selfish; they will ask rather what was the life of the people or the development of the constitution. The extracts here collected will, it is hoped, be interesting to both classes. Battles and campaigns take up, it is true, the larger part of the book, but this is fitting; for it tells the story of the great struggle with the kings of France which had such far-reaching consequences to the two countries. But the constitutional and social results of the period have also been as far as

PREFACE.

possible illustrated. Narratives of Crecy and Poitiers, of Halidon Hill and Neville's Cross will be found here; but so will also the statutes for the protection of the English church and concerning taxation and treason, some account of the Black Death and its consequences, some glimpses into the history of industry and the life of the universities.

In the appendix are given a description of the authors herein used and various genealogical tables; it may be well to mention also that the headings to the extracts are in almost every case taken from the original authorities. It remains only for the editor to express his gratitude to Miss Lucy Hill for much careful assistance and many a happy suggestion.

Lincoln College, February, 1887.

EDWARD III & HIS WARS

1327.— The accession of Edward III.

Murimuth, 51-53.

(Queen Isabella and the young prince Edward, who had been in France negotiating about Guienne, returned to England in September, 1326, accompanied by Mortimer and a force of Hainaulters, their declared purpose being to put an end to the misrule of the Despensers. They met with no opposition; the Despensers were hanged; and Edward II. was imprisoned at Kenilworth.)

The queen (Isabella) . . . immediately after Epiphany, caused a parliament to be held, in which it was ordained, on behalf of the whole realm, that three bishops, two earls, two abbots, and four barons, from each county of England two knights, also from London and the other cities and great towns, and especially from the Cinque Ports, a certain number of persons, should be sent to the king. (Edward II.) at Kenilworth, and should tell him and diligently require him to resign the royal dignity and crown, and permit his eldest son to reign in his stead; otherwise they would return him their homages and elect another as their king. When he heard this, the king replied, with weeping and lamentation, that it grieved him much that he had deserved so ill of his people; but, since it could not be otherwise, said he, he was glad that his son had been thus received by the whole people, and that he should succeed him and reign in his stead. Then the delegates, returning to the parliament at London, reported the king's answers fully, more fully indeed than they had been given; and when they had heard them the whole community of the realm at once admitted the young Edward as king, and on the first day of February caused him to be crowned at Westminster by archbishop Walter. . . Moreover, such and so great a dowry was assigned to the queen that scarcely a third part of the realm remained to the king, her son.

SEAL OF EDWARD III.

1327.—Charter granting the township of Southwark to the citizens of London.

Inserted in the London *Liber Custumarum* (in *Munimenta Gildhallæ Londoniensis*, ii. 435. Rolls Series).

(This important grant to the citizens of London was probably given as a reward for their support in the recent revolution.)

Edward, by the grace of God, king of England, lord of Ireland, and duke of Aquitaine, to all to whom the present letters may come, greeting.

Know that whereas our beloved citizens of our city of London, by their petition shewn to us and our council in our present parliament at Westminster assembled, have given us to understand that felons, robbers, and divers other malefactors and disturbers of the peace, who have committed in that city and elsewhere murders, robberies, and divers other felonies, secretly leave that city after committing such felonies and take refuge in the township of Southwark, where they cannot be arrested by the officers of the said city, and are there publicly received; and so, from want of due punishment, they are made the more bold in committing like felonies; and have besought us, for the preservation of our peace in the said city, and bridling the malice of these criminals, to grant them the said township, to have to themselves, their heirs and successors for ever, in return for a ferm (annual payment) due therefor to be annually paid to us at our Exchequer —We, having consideration to the foregoing, by the consent of the prelates, earls, barons, and commons of our realm in the present parliament, grant for us and our heirs, to the same citizens, the said township of Southwark, with what thereto pertains, to have and to hold to them, their heirs and successors, the citizens of the said city, of us and our heirs for ever, paying to us annually at the Exchequer of us and our heirs, at the accustomed terms, the ferm thereof due and accustomed. In witness of which we have caused these, our Letters Patent, to be drawn up. Witness myself at Westminster, the sixth day of March, the first year of our reign.

1327.—Here the history speaketh of the manner of the Scots and how they can war.

Froissart, ch. 17 (I. § 28).   *Jehan le Bel*, ch. 10.

(Robert Bruce took advantage of the troubles in England upon the deposition of Edward II. to break the truce and send an army to ravage the northern counties. Jehan le Bel accompanied the English force against them, and thus describes the Scotch troops.)

These Scottish men are right hardy and sore travailing in harness and in wars. For when they will enter into England, within a day and a night they will drive their whole host twenty-four miles. For they are all a-horse-back, without it be the camp-followers who come on foot. The knights and squires are well horsed, and the common people and others on little hackneys and geldings; and they carry with them no carts nor chariots, for the diversities of the mountains that they must pass through in the county of Northumberland. They take with them no purveyance of bread or wine; for their usage and soberness is such, in the time of war, that they will pass in the journey a great long time with flesh half sodden, without bread, and drink of the river water without wine; and they neither care for pots nor pans, for they seethe beasts in their own skins. They are ever sure to find plenty of beasts in the country that they will pass through. Therefore they carry with them none other purveyance, but on their horse between the saddle and the panel they truss a broad plate of metal, and behind the saddle they will have a little sack full of oatmeal to the intent that, when they have eaten of the sodden flesh, then they lay this plate on the fire and mix a little oatmeal, and when the plate is hot they cast of the thin paste thereon, and so make a little cake in manner of a cracknel or biscuit, and that they eat to comfort withal their stomachs. Wherefore it is no great marvel though they make greater journeys than other people do. And in this manner were the Scots entered into the said country, and wasted and burnt all about as they went, and took a great number of the beasts. They were to the number of four thousand men of arms, knights and squires, mounted on good horses, and other ten thousand men of war were armed after their manner, right hardy and fierce, mounted on little hackneys, the which were never tied nor kept at hard meat, but let go to pasture in the fields and bushes.

1327.—How the English sought the Scots and knew not where they were.

Froissart, ch. 18 (I. §§ 30, 31, 32). *Jehan le Bel*, ch. 11, 12.

(The English, being unable to find the Scots, tried to cut off their retreat.)

. . . It was determined by great advice and counsel that all the host should remove at midnight, and make haste in the morning, to the intent to stop the passage of the river of Tyne from the Scots, whereby they should be advised by force, either to fight with them, or else to abide still in England to their great danger and loss. And to this conclusion all the host was accorded, and so supped and lodged as well as they might that night, and every man was warned to be ready at the first sounding of the trumpet, and at the second blast every man to arm himself without delay, and at the third every man quickly to mount on his horse and to draw under his own standard and banner, and every man to take with him but one loaf of bread, and to truss it behind him on his horse. It was also determined that they should leave behind them all their loose harness and all manner of carriages and provisions; for they thought surely to fight with the Scots the next day, whatsoever danger they were in, thinking to jeopard either to win or to lose all. And thus it was ordained and so it was accomplished, for about midnight every man was ready apparelled. Few had slept but little, and yet they had sore travailed the day before. Great haste as they made, ere they were arranged in battle-array the day began to appear. Then they advanced forward in all haste, through mountains, valleys, and rocks, and through many evil passages without any plain country. And on the highest of these hills and on the plain of these valleys there were marvellous great marshes and dangerous passages, that it was great marvel that much people had not been lost; for they rode ever still forward and never tarried one for another; for whosoever fell in any of these marshes with much pain could they get any aid to help them out again. So that in diverse places there were many lost and especially horses and carriages. And often times in the day there was cried alarm, for it was said ever that the foremost company of their host were fighting with their enemies; so that the hindermost thought it had been true, wherefore they hasted them over rocks and stones and mountains with helm and shield ready apparelled to fight, with spear and sword ready in hand without tarrying for father, brother, or companion. And when they had thus run forth often times in the day the space of half-a-mile together toward the crying, thinking it had been their enemies, they were deceived, for the cry ever arose by the raising of harts, hinds, and other savage beasts that were seen by them in the forward; after the which beasts they made such shouting and crying, that they that came after thought they had been fighting with their enemies. Thus rode forth all that day the young king of England by mountains and deserts without finding any highway, town, or village. And when it was again night they came to the river Tyne. . . .

(They crossed the river, and waited in the rain and with little food till the middle of next day; but the Scots did not appear.) About noon some poor folks of the country were found, and they said how they were then fourteen miles from Newcastle-upon-Tyne and eleven miles from Carlisle. . . . . And when this was shewn to the king and to the lords of his council, immediately were sent thither horses and sumpters to fetch thence some purveyance; and there was a cry in the king's name made in the town of Newcastle that whosoever would bring bread or wine or any other victual, should be paid therefor

immediately at a good price, and they should be conducted to the host in safeguard; for it was published openly that the king and his host would not depart from the place they were in till they had some tidings where their enemies were. And the next day by noon such as had been sent for victual returned again to the host, with such purveyance as they could get, and that was not over much; and with them came other folks of the country with little nags charged with bread, evil baked in panniers, and small pear wine in barrels, and other victual, to sell in the host, whereby great part of the host were well refreshed and eased. And thus they continued, day by day, the space of eight days, awaiting every day the returning again of the Scots, who knew no more where the English host lay than they knew where the Scots were; so each of them were ignorant of the other. . . . . .
Thus three days and three nights they were in manner without bread, wine, candle, or light, fodder or forage, or any manner of provision either for horse or man. And after the space of four days a loaf of bread was sold for six pennies the which was worth but one penny, and a gallon of wine for six groats that was worth but six pennies. And yet for all that, there was such rage of famine that each took victuals out of others' hands, whereby there arose divers battles and strifes between sundry companions; and yet beside all these mischiefs it never ceased to rain all the whole week, whereby their saddles, panels, and saddlestraps were all rotten and broken

and most part of their horses hurt on their backs; nor they had not wherewith to shoe them that were unshod; nor they had nothing to cover themselves withal from the rain and cold, but green bushes and their armour. Nor they had nothing to make fire withal but green boughs, the which would not burn because of the rain. . . . .

(The Scots not appearing, the English recrossed the river and tried to find them.)

. . . Again, the fourth day they rode forth in like manner till it was about the hour of three, and there came a squire fast riding toward the king and said, "An it like your grace, I have brought you perfect tidings of the Scots, your enemies; surely they be within three miles of you, lodged on a great mountain, abiding there for you. . . . Sir, this that I show you is of truth, for I approached so near to them that I was taken prisoner, and brought before the lords of their host, and there I shewed them tidings of you, and how that ye seek for them, to the intent to have battle, and the lords did quit me my ransom and prison, when I had shewed them how our grace had promised a hundred pounds sterling of rent to him that brought first tiding of them to you; and they made me to promise that I should not rest until I had shewed you these tidings, for they said they had as great desire to fight with you as you had with them." . . . .

(The English followed this squire and found the Scots strongly posted on a hill with a river running in front, and refusing to leave their strong position.)

. . . And there were heralds of arms sent to the Scots, giving them knowledge that if they would come and pass the river to fight with them in the plain field, they would draw back from the river and give them sufficient place to arrange their lines of battle, either the same day or else the next, as they should choose themselves, or else to let them do likewise and they would come over to them. And when the Scots heard this they took counsel among themselves; and anon they answered the heralds how they would do neither the one nor the other, and said, "Sirs, your king and his lords see well how we be here in this realm, and have burnt and wasted the country as we have passed through; and if they be displeased therewith, let them amend it when they will, for here we will abide so long as it shall please us." . . . . . And between the day and the night, they made a marvellous great noise with blowing of horns all at once, that it seemed properly that all the devils of hell had been there. Thus these two hosts were lodged there that night, the which was St. Peter's night, in the beginning of August, the year of our Lord, 1327. . . . .

(After facing one another for five days, the Scots departed in the night; the English again found them, and the same comedy was played.)

The first night that the English host was thus lodged on the second mountain, the lord James Douglas took with him about two hundred men of arms, and passed the river far off from the host so that he was not perceived; and suddenly he brake into the English host about midnight, crying, "Douglas! Douglas! Ye shall all die, thieves of England"; and he slew or seized 300 men, some in their beds and some scant ready; and he strake his horse with the spurs, and came to the king's own tent, always crying "Douglas!" and strake asunder two or three cords of the king's tent, and so departed, and in the retreat he lost some of his men. . . . .

(Again the Scots eluded them.)

Then the English lords said it were but a folly to follow the Scots, for they saw well they could not overtake them. . . . . And divers of the English host mounted on their horses, and passed over the river and came to the mountain where the Scots had been, and there they found more than 500 great beasts ready slain, because the Scots could not drive them before their host, and because that the Englishmen should have but small profit of them; also there they found 300 cauldrons made of beast's skins with the hair still on them, strained on stakes over the fire, full of water and full of flesh to be sodden; and more than a thousand spits full of flesh to be roasted; and more than ten thousand old shoes made of new leather with the hair still on them, the which the Scots had left behind them; also there they found five poor Englishmen, bound fast to certain trees and some of their legs broken; these they loosed and let go and then they returned again.

By that time all the host was dislodged; and it was ordained by the king, and by the advice of his council, that the whole host should follow the marshal's banners and draw homeward into England.

1327.—The murder of Edward II.

Murimuth, 53-55.

Because it seemed to some that lord Edward, father of the king, was too delicately treated at Kenilworth, it was ordered that lord Thomas of Berkeley and lord John of Mautravers should have the custody of him; wherefore, about Palm Sunday, he was secretly taken to Berkeley. And, because they feared that some would come to free him, he was taken from that place by night to divers places, viz., to Corf and to some other secret places, but finally they brought him back to Berkeley, so that he could scarce know where he was; and the lord of Berkeley, who behaved humanely towards him, had always charge of him for one month, and the next month lord John Mautravers, who behaved towards him differently. The queen, indeed, sent him delicate raiment and courteous letters, but would not see him, pretending that the community of the realm would not permit her. He had an allowance, viz., a hundred marks a month; and so at Berkeley and elsewhere, not where he pleased but where this John Mautravers pleased, he lived as best he could until the time to be mentioned below. . . . Afterwards, on the 21st of September, in the year of Our Lord, 1327, Edward, king of England, died in the castle of Berkeley, wherein, as I have before said, he was imprisoned or unwillingly detained. And, although many abbots, priors, knights, burgesses of Bristol and Gloucester, had been summoned to see that his body was unhurt, and had superficially seen it, yet it was commonly said that he had been killed as a precaution by the order of the lords John Mautravers and Thomas of Gorneye, because these two and some others fled; but Thomas of Gorneye was three years afterwards recognised and captured at Marseilles by the procurement of a certain lady of England, and was sent to England to suffer the penalty of his misdeeds, but he was beheaded upon the sea upon some pretext; lest perchance he should accuse magnates and great prelates in England of consent and connivance at the King's death; but lord John Mautravers betook himself to Germany, and there he abode and abides still up to the present date.

1328.—How king Edward was married to my lady Philippa of Hainault.

Froissart, ch. 19 (1. §§ 38-9).   *Jehan le Bel*, ch. 14.

It was not long after that the king and the queen his mother, the earl of Kent his uncle, the earl of Lancaster, sir Roger Mortimer, and all the barons of England who were of the king's council, sent a bishop and two knights bannerets with two notable clerks to sir John of Hainault, praying him to be a mean that their lord, the young king of England, might have in marriage one of the daughters of the earl of Hainault his brother, named Philippa; for the king and all the nobles of the realm had rather have her than any other lady for the love of him. Sir John of Hainault, lord Beaumont, feasted and honoured greatly these ambassadors, and brought them to Valenciennes to the earl his brother, who honourably received them and made them such cheer that it were over long here to rehearse. And when they had shown the contents of their message, the earl said, "Sirs, I thank greatly the king, your prince, and the queen his mother, and all other lords of England, since they have sent such sufficient personages as ye be to do me such honour as to treat for the marriage, to the which request I am well agreed, if our holy father, the pope, will consent thereto"; with the which answer these ambassadors were right well content. Then they sent two knights and two clerks immediately to the pope to Avignon, to obtain a dispensation for this marriage; for, without the pope's license they might not marry, for in the lineage of France they were so near of kin as at the third degree, for the two mothers were cousins german, issued of two brethren. And when these ambassadors were come to the pope, and their requests and considerations well heard, our holy father the pope, with all the whole college, consented to this marriage, and so feasted them. And then they departed and came again to Valenciennes with their bulls. Then this marriage was concluded and affirmed on both parties; . . . . there this princess was married, by a sufficient procuration brought from the king of England; and after all feasts and triumphs done, then this young queen entered into the sea at Wysant, and arrived with all her company at Dover. And sir John of Hainault, lord Beaumont, her uncle, did conduct her to the city of London where there was made great feast. . . . . The English chronicle saith the marriage and coronation of the queen was done at York, with much honour, the Sunday in the even of the conversion of S. Paul, in the year of our Lord 1327. (N.S. 1328.).

1328, March.—Peace with Scotland.

Chronicle of Lanercost, p. 261.

Then the king of England (hearing of the death of his uncle without heir, and deeming himself of right the next heir to reign in France, yet fearing that those of France would not suffer him, but would choose another of the royal blood to be their king, as indeed they immediately did, the son, to wit, of Charles, the uncle of the late king), by the most evil advice of his mother and lord Roger of Mortimer, who were the chief leaders of the king who was scarce fifteen years old, was compelled to give up to the Scots, by his public charter, every exaction, right, and claim lately made of chief lordship over the realm of Scotland, for himself and his heirs for ever, without their doing homage to the kings of England. He gave up also to them the piece of the Cross of Christ, which the Scots call the Blackrood, and likewise an instrument or charter of subjection or doing of homage to the kings of England, with the seals of all the magnates of Scotland hanging to it, which they had given to the king's grandfather, and which the Scots on account of its many seals called Ragman. But the stone of Scone, whereon the kings of Scotland were wont to be placed at their coronation, the Londoners would by no means send away. All these the famous king Edward, son of Henry, had caused to be brought from Scotland when he brought the Scots beneath his sway. Moreover the young king gave his younger sister, lady Joan of the Tower, in marriage to David, son of Robert Bruce, king of Scotland, who was then a boy of five years old, as his mother the queen of England had advised, who at that time ruled the whole kingdom. And the marriage was solemnly celebrated at Berwick, on the Sunday next before the feast of S. Mary Magdalen.

1328.—How king Robert Bruce of Scotland died.

Froissart, ch. 20 (1. §§ 40-41). *Jehan le Bel*, ch. 15-16.

In the meantime it fortuned that king Robert of Scotland was right sore aged and feeble; for he was greatly charged with the great sickness (leprosy), so that there was no way with him but death. And when he felt that his end drew near, he sent for such barons and lords of his realm as he trusted best, and shewed them how there was no remedy with him, but he must needs leave this transitory life; commanding them on the faith and truth that they owed him, truly to keep the realm and aid the young prince David his son; and that when he was of age they should obey him and crown him king, and marry him in such a manner as was convenient for his estate. Then he called to him the gentle knight, sir James Douglas, and said before all the lords: " Sir James, my dear friend, ye know well that I have had much ado in my days to uphold and sustain the right of this realm; and when I had most ado I made a solemn vow, the which as yet I have not accomplished, whereof I am right sorry; the which was, if I might achieve and make an end of all my wars, so that I might once have brought this realm in rest and peace, then I promised in my mind to have gone and warred on Christ's enemies, the adversaries of our holy Christian faith. To this purpose mine heart has ever intended, but our Lord would not consent thereto; for I have had so much ado in my days, and now in my last enterprise I have taken such a malady that I cannot escape. And since it is that my body cannot go nor achieve that my heart desireth, I will send the heart instead of the body to accomplish my vow. And because I know in all my realm no knight more valiant than ye be nor of body so well furnished to accomplish my vow instead of myself, therefore I require you, my own dear especial friend, that ye will take on you this voyage for the love of me, and to acquit my soul against my Lord God. For I trust so much in your nobleness and truth that, an ye will take it on you, I doubt not but that ye shall achieve it, and I declare then shall I die in more ease and quiet so that it be done in such manner as I shall declare unto you. I will that, as soon as I shall be passed out of this world, ye take my heart out of my body and embalm it; and take of my treasure as ye shall think sufficient for that enterprise, both for yourself and such company as ye will take with you; and present my heart to the Holy Sepulchre where our Lord lay, seeing that my body cannot come there. And take with you such company and purveyance as shall be appertaining to your estate. And wheresoever ye come, let it be known how ye carry with you the heart of king Robert of Scotland at his request and desire, to be presented to the Holy Sepulchre." Then all the lords that heard these words wept for pity. And when this knight sir James Douglas might speak for weeping, he said "Ah! gentle and noble king, a hundred times I thank your grace for the great honour that ye do to me, since of so noble and great treasure ye give me in charge; and, sir, I shall do with a glad heart all that ye have commanded me to the best of my true power; howbeit I am not worthy nor sufficient to achieve such a noble enterprise." Then the king said "Ah! gentle knight I thank you, so that ye will promise to do it." "Sir," said the knight, "I shall do it undoubtedly, by the faith that I owe to God and to the order of knighthood." "Then I thank you," said the king, "for now shall

I die in more ease of my mind, since that I know that the most worthy and sufficient knight of my realm shall achieve for me that which I could never attain unto." And thus, soon after this, noble Robert de Bruce, king of Scotland, passed away out of this uncertain world. And his heart was taken out of his body and embalmed, and honourably he was interred in the Abbey of Dunfermline in the year of our Lord God, 1328, the 7th day of the month of November.

And when the spring-time began, then sir James Douglas purveyed him with that which appertained for his enterprise and took his ship at the port of Montrose in Scotland, and sailed into Flanders to Sluys, to hear tidings and to know if there were any noble men in that country that would go to Jerusalem, to the intent to have more company. And he lay still at Sluys the space of 12 days ere he departed; but he would never come a-land, but kept still his ship and always kept his state and behaviour with great triumph, with trumpets and clarions as though he had been king of Scots himself. And in his company there was a knight banneret, and eight other knights of the realm of Scotland and twenty-four young squires and gentlemen to serve him. And all his vessels were of gold and silver, pots, basins, ewers, dishes, flagons, barrels, cups, and all other things. And all such as would come and see him, they were well served with two manner of wines and divers manner of spices, all manner of people according to their degrees. And when he had thus

tarried there the space of twelve days, he heard
reported that Alfonso, king of Spain, made war
against a Saracen king of Granada. Then he
thought to join himself to the Spanish king, thinking
surely he could not bestow his time more nobly than
to war against God's enemies. And that enterprise
done, then he thought to go forth to Jerusalem and
to achieve that he was charged with. And so he
departed and took the sea towards Spain, and arrived
at the port of Valencia the great. Then he went
straight to the king of Spain who held his host
against the Saracen king of Granada, and they were
near together on the frontiers of his land. And
within a while after that this knight, sir James
Douglas, was come to the king of Spain, on a day
the king issued out into the field to approach nearer
to his enemies. And the king of Granada issued
out in like wise on his part, so that each king might
see the other with all their banners displayed. Then
they arranged their battles each against the other.
Then sir James Douglas drew out on the one side
with all his company to the intent to show his
prowess the better. And when he saw these battles
thus ranged on both parties, and saw that the battle
of the king of Spain began somewhat to advance
toward their enemies he thought then verily that
they should soon assemble together to fight at hand
strokes; and then he thought rather to be with the
foremost than with the hindermost, and struck his
horse with his spurs, and all his company also, and
dashed into the battle of the king of Granada,

crying, "Douglas, Douglas!" weening that the king of Spain and his host had followed, but they did not; wherefore he was dismayed, for the Spanish host stood still. And so this gentle knight was enclosed and all his company with the Saracens, where he did marvels in arms, but finally he could not endure, so that he and all his company were slain.

1328-9. — Of the struggle between Mortimer and Lancaster.

Knighton, 2554.

At Salisbury, queen Isabella and Roger of Mortimer made new earls, namely, John of Eltham, earl of Cornwall; Roger of Mortimer, earl of March; Edmund Butler, earl of Ormond. All these, with their adherents, brought together a great army to Isabella the queen against Henry earl of Lancaster and the other magnates of the realm who had not been consenting to their nefarious deeds. And they rode with force and arms upon the lands of the said earl, and came to Leicester with a great army of English and Welsh on the fourth of January, and they remained in Leicester and in the country around eight days, and spoiled the country everywhere, woods, parks, vineyards, pools, and fishponds, and took away with them everything, whether precious or not, that their hands could find, gold, silver, corn, tools, beds, tables, arms, clothes, game and cattle, sheep and oxen, geese and hens, and church ornaments, leaving nothing that they could find in churches or elsewhere, as if it had been in time of war between kingdoms. And all this as an insult to the earl of Lancaster, who was then coming from the eastern counties with a large force, wishing to meet them, having in his following the magnates who had been with Thomas earl of Lancaster, to wit the earl of Norfolk, Edmund earl of Kent, his brother and uncle of the king, the bishops of London and Winchester, the lord Wake, the lord Beaumont, Hugh of Audley, the lord Thomas Rosselyne, and many others. And when these magnates had made themselves ready for the attack, since they distrusted Roger Mortimer, by whose counsel and prompting the king had taken offence against certain of his faithful lieges, the two uncles of the king, Thomas and Edmund, left the earl and joined the king's mother and Roger Mortimer. . . . . . Earl Henry, trusting in their fidelity, had taken his stand in a field near Bedford, and fixed his tents, purposing to join battle with Roger of Mortimer and his adherents; but, owing to this betrayal, he humbly submitted himself to the king in the field in the presence of the whole army. And there it was agreed, in the presence of Simon archbishop of Canterbury and other bishops and many of the magnates of the realm, that all evils should be remedied in the next parliament, and this lest, perchance, all the commons should rise and make common cause with the earl.

1330.—Of the death of Edmund of Kent.

Knighton, 2555.

In the year of grace, 1330, and in the 4th year of the reign of king Edward, the king held a parliament at Winchester. In which it was laid to the charge of Edmund earl of Kent by Isabella the mother, and Roger Mortimer and others of their party, that he had endeavoured and taken great pains, contrary to his duty to the king, to free Edward, his brother, formerly king of England, from the castle of Berkeley, to the prejudice and hurt of the crown. Wherefore the said Edmund was taken and imprisoned and condemned to the penalty of beheading; and so stood outside the gate of the castle, awaiting death until the hour of vespers, because no one was willing to behead him, for the pity they had for him, for he had been condemned without common consent. At last came a ribald scoundrel from the Marshalsey, and, to gain his own life, beheaded him on Monday in the vigil of S. Cuthbert.

1330.—Of the fall of Roger Mortimer.

Knighton, 2555-7.

. . . . Then a rumour began to spread through the whole of England of the malignity and cruelty of Isabella, the king's mother, and of the many seditions of Roger Mortimer. In the first place that they encouraged the Scots to the great hurt and disgrace of the king and kingdom of England, and how that she had put to death king Edward, once her husband, and how many evils were done in the realm by their counsel and aid, and how many evil works were concealed by their help. Wherefore the king, by the secret advice of his friends, determined to break up their fellowship, lest worse or like should at any time arise by their act or counsel. For they were becoming so strong in the land that the whole kingdom seemed in peril of falling. Then the king held his council at Nottingham in the season of Michaelmas, with almost all the magnates of the realm. Wherein the king, being more wholesomely taught by wiser counsel of their fraud and malice, and seeing the danger as well past as future and present from the said Isabella and Mortimer, was much moved at heart; and so on the Wednesday on the morrow of S. Luke, the king with a picked following on a dark night made his way by a certain subterranean passage from the town of Nottingham into the castle, and came into the chamber of his mother, Isabella, and found there near her in another chamber Roger Mortimer and Henry, bishop of Lincoln. And immediately the king ordered Roger to be apprehended and put in safe custody until the morrow. On the morrow he caused all his adherents scattered through the whole town to be apprehended. . . . . . And in the capture of Roger Mortimer, Hugh of Tryplington, a knight and seneschal of the king's household, was killed by Roger Mortimer in the entry of the king into their chamber. Isabella, the king's mother, was adjudged to lose all her lands, and with difficulty escaped the sentence of death, this being refrained from because she was the king's mother and on account of the king's reverence. And it was ordained that each year 3,000 marks should be taken from the chest of the king for her sustenance, and that she should dwell where the king should appoint. .... Then the king ordered the earls, barons, and other magnates of the realm, to pass just sentence on Roger Mortimer. These all consulting together came and said that all the above articles witnessed against Roger were true and notorious, and known to all the people of the land, especially the article touching the death of the king at Berkeley; wherefore it was determined and adjudged that the said Roger should be drawn and hanged at London. His body hung bare on the gallows two days and two nights, and was then buried at the convent of the Franciscans at London.

1331.—Protection to a Flemish weaver.

Rymer, Fœdera, ii. 823.

(This illustrates the policy of Edward III. to encourage the settlement of foreign weavers in England, to which was chiefly due the rapid growth of the cloth manufacture in England from this time.)

The king to all bailiffs, etc., to whom these letters may come, greeting. Know that, whereas John Kempe, of Flanders, weaver of woollen cloths, has come to dwell within our realm of England for the sake of exercising his craft therein and of instructing and informing those who wish to learn the same, and has brought with him certain men and servants and apprentices of that craft:

We take this John, his men, servants, and apprentices aforesaid, together with all their goods and chattels, into our protection, and we promise to other men of that craft, as well as to dyers and fullers, wishing to come from across the sea to dwell within our kingdom for the same cause, that similar letters shall be granted. . . . .

Witness the king, at Lincoln, the 28th day of July.

(Similar letters of protection were afterwards frequently issued, *e.g.* to two Brabant weavers who had settled at York in 1336, to weavers from Zealand in 1337.)

1333.—Of the battle of Halidon Hill.

Chronicle of Lanercost, p. 273.

(The Scotch government having refused to reinstate those English lords who had lands in Scotland, they induced Edward Balliol, son of king John Balliol, to make an attempt to gain the crown in the summer of 1332. At first he was entirely successful; the regent was defeated at Duplin Moor, and Balliol was crowned at Scone. But in a few months he had to take refuge in England. Edward's sympathies had long been on the side of Balliol; border frays gave him an excuse for breaking the peace, and he joined Balliol in besieging Berwick.)

The king of England, hearing that the Scots had entered his land, and had done all the evils of which we have spoken, although he himself had not yet broken the peace and concord made between him and David, son of lord Robert of Bruce, who had married Edward's sister, who was with him in Scotland, approached Berwick about the festival of

the apostles Philip and James (May 1.) in order to
vanquish the Scots and assist the king of Scotland,
having with him his own brother John of Eltham,
and many other noble earls, barons, knights, and
squires, and thirty thousand picked men, the king
of Scotland being then besieging that town. And
within the week after Ascension Day (May 20) the
two kings with their army made a vigorous assault
on the said town, but those within (on account
of the strength and height of the wall, which the
father of the king of England had caused to be
built when the town was in his power) bravely
resisted and manfully defended themselves, so that
the English could not force an entrance, although
they continued the siege. Then on the 14th of
the calends of August, to wit on the vigil of S.
Margaret, virgin and martyr (July 19), after breakfast,
came the Scots in great multitude to their destruction,
marching in three lines towards the town of Berwick,
against the two kings and their armies then besieging
it, who however were ready and informed of their
coming. But the Scots who marched in the first
line were so wounded in the face and blinded by
the multitude of the English arrows, in this battle
as in the previous one at Gledenmoor, that they
could not help themselves, and soon began to
turn their faces away from the blows of the arrows
and fall. Even after the English and the Scotch
alike were drawn up in triple line, the king
of Scotland being in the hindermost, the Scots
turned to meet and do battle with the line of him

who, not unjustly, was seeking his right to the kingdom. However, as it is said, their first line was soon thrown into confusion and overcome by his (Balliol's) army before the rest began to fight. And, while he scattered the first division, the other two wings fell in battle before the English. Those of the Scots who were behind took to flight on foot, but the English followed them on horseback down the the different lanes, and knocked down the wretched fugitives with staves with iron teeth. On that day were killed of the Scots, as was said, 7 earls, namely, those of Ross, of Lennox, of Carrick, of Sutherland, and three others, and 27 bannerets, and 36,320 foot soldiers, though, according to some, fewer, according to others, many more. Among others also fell lord Archibald of Douglas, who had been the chief cause of their coming to this destruction; had not night soon fallen, many more would have been killed.

Before the Scotch army had got as far as Berwick a monk, who was in their company and heard their deliberations, cried to them "Proceed no further! Let us all return; for I see Christ crucified coming against you in the air from Berwick with brandished spear." But they, like proud and obstinate men, confiding in their numbers, which were twice as great as the English, hardened their hearts and would not return. This was told by one of the Scots, who was made a knight just before the battle, and was captured in the battle and put to ransom, adding that two hundred and three Scots were made knights before the battle, and none of them

escaped death except himself and four only with
him.

(Berwick gave itself up to Edward; the national party in
Scotland seemed crushed; and the young David Bruce took
refuge in France.)

1334.—Of the homage done by Edward of Balliol.

Chronicle of Lanercost, p. 277.

On the nineteenth day of June, that is to say on the
feast of the holy martyrs, Gervasius and Prothasius, at
Newcastle-upon-Tyne, came the king of Scotland, and
the earls of Athol and Dunbar, Mar and Buchan; and
then in the presence of the two English earls—the
king's brothers, the earl of Cornwall and the earl of
Warrenne—and these four Scotch earls, and of the
archbishop of York and the bishops of Durham and
Carlisle, and an almost innumerable multitude of
clergy and people, the king of Scotland, Edward of
Balliol, did his homage to his lord Edward the third,
king of England, to hold the kingdom of Scotland
of him, as of his chief lord, and of his heirs and
successors for ever. And because the king of England
had assisted him to re-enter and take possession of
his kingdom of Scotland, from which he had been
expelled by the Scots for a time, and had incurred
great expenses, the king of Scotland yielded to him
five Scotch counties which are nearest to the English
March—namely, the counties of Berwick and Roxburgh, Peebles and Dumfries, and the town of Hadington and the town of Sedburgh, with its castle,
and the forests of Selkirk and Ettrick and Sedburgh,

so that all these should be separated from the crown of Scotland and annexed to the crown of England for ever. Thus there did not remain to the king of Scotland this side the Scotch sea,* more than five counties, to wit, Ayr, Dunbarton, Lanark, Stirling, and Wigtown in Galway beyond the Firth. All the above said were publicly confirmed by oath and writing and fit witnesses, and this being done the king returned to England.

1334.—Order against Oxford students seceding to Stamford.

Rymer, Fœdera, ii. 891.

(Owing to the frequent conflicts between Northerners and Southerners at Oxford, many students had withdrawn to Stamford, which seemed likely to become a formidable rival to Oxford and Cambridge.)

The king, to the sheriff of Lincoln, greeting. Whereas we are given to understand that many masters and scholars of our university of Oxford, under colour of certain dissensions lately, as it is said, arisen in that university, and with other idle pretexts, withdrawing themselves from that university, presume to betake themselves to the town of Stamford, and there carry on their studies and perform scholastic exercises, having by no means sought our assent or license; which, if it were tolerated, would manifestly turn not only to our contempt and disgrace but also to the dispersion of our said university;

* The Firth of Forth.

We, unwilling that schools or studies should in any wise be carried on elsewhere within our realm than in places where there are now universities, order and firmly enjoin you to go in person to the said town of Stamford, and there and elsewhere within your bailiwick where it is expedient, cause it to be publicly proclaimed with our authority, and prohibition made, that any should carry on study or perform scholastic exercises elsewhere than in our said universities, under penalty of forfeiting to us all they can forfeit ; and cause us, without delay, to be informed distinctly and openly, in our chancery, and under your seal, of the names of those whom you find disobeying, after this proclamation and prohibition ;

For we will that speedy justice be done as is fitting to all and everyone ready to bring their complaints of any violence or injury done to them at the said city of Oxford, before our justices there, specially deputed for this purpose.

Witness the king at Windsor, the second day of August.

By the king and council.

(This vigorous measure was successful, but not until a writ had been issued next year ordering the seizure of the books of the disobedient.)

1334-6.—Unsuccessful expeditions of Edward into Scotland.

Murimuth, pp. 75-80.

(The cession of the Lothians by Balliol caused him to be again driven out. The following is a short account of Edward's vain endeavours to re-conquer Scotland for him.)

When the news came to the parliament that the Scots had all revolted and had taken prisoner the lord Richard Talbot and six other knights, and had slain many foot-soldiers, the king declared that he would go to Scotland to bridle the malice of the Scots; and the people granted to him the fifteenth penny of lay property, and from the cities and burgesses the tenth penny, and the clergy granted a tenth.

Also in the same parliament our lord the king consented to go to the Holy Land at his own charge, yet did not fix any certain time for beginning his journey, but ordered that the archbishop of Canterbury should be sent to the pope and to the king of France to agree about the time; in order that the two kings with their forces, should set out at the same time; but nothing was ever really done. . . .

Soon after Michaelmas the king marched to the Scotch borders, and wintered in those parts; and having heard that the earl of Athol had treacherously joined the Scots, and that they were besieging the lord Henry of Beaumont in a certain castle, he entered Scotland and caused the siege to be raised; and kept Christmas at Roxburgh. . . . .

The archbishop of Canterbury returned about Epiphany (1335). . . . And soon after Epiphany, the king of France sent ambassadors to the king of England, to wit the bishop of Avranches and a certain baron, to bring about a peace with the

Scotch, and they waited in England till the middle of Lent; and then at Nottingham a truce was granted until the feast of S. John the Baptist, in order that the parliament might deal meanwhile with these matters and others touching the state of the realm. In this parliament held at York, it was ordained that the king and the earls and the barons with their forces should enter Scotland and cross the Scotch sea; which soon afterwards was done. But the Scotch, unwilling to array battle in the open, pretended that they wished peace; and afterwards, about Michaelmas, many made peace, especially the earl of Athol; but others refused; so that soon after the earl of Moray was captured at Edinburgh and sent to be imprisoned in England, and the lord Richard Talbot was redeemed for two thousand marks. But the earl of Athol, wishing to shew that he had really joined the English, rode against the Scots to besiege a castle and suddenly, having but a small force with him, fell among the enemy who were greatly superior in number; and willing not to yield but to fight was slain with thirteen persons of less estate after Michaelmas. The king, however, still remained on the Scotch borders and likewise also the ambassadors of the pope and the king of France, waiting to bring about some peace or long truce, to us useless. . . . This year the king had a tenth from the burgesses, a fifteenth from his other subjects, and a tenth from the clergy. And about Whitsuntide (1336) the king held a parliament at Northampton, where he left the prelates and others to treat, and he himself secretly rode towards Scotland, with very few followers, as far as Berwick; and thence taking a few troops he rode to the town of S. John (Perth), where he found his forces, who were surprised and wondered at his arrival. He caused that town to be fortified with ditches and walls, and sent his earls with the king of Scotland through the country, to see if they could join battle with the Scots; but none dared to await them, but lay in hiding in the mountains, marshes, and forests. . . . . In October died John of Eltham, earl of Cornwall, brother of the king of England, and this was in Scotland and not in battle. Also this year, our lord the king caused to be taken in every cathedral church all the money collected and placed there for the crusade. Also, this year, the pope recalled the tenth for six years which had been granted for the crusade, because the king of France put off his journey to the Holy Land too much, and the pope desired that what had been paid should be returned; but nothing was returned in England because the clergy granted it to the king.

1337.—Prohibition of the export of wool.

Murimuth, p. 81.

(This was probably intended partly to encourage the rising cloth manufacture in England, but partly also to coerce the earl of Flanders into joining Edward against Philip of Valois.)

The king summoned his parliament for the Monday after the feast of S. Matthew the apostle, and in this he made his eldest son, duke of Cornwall, the lord Henry, son of the earl of Lancaster, earl of Derby, the lord William of Bohun, earl of Northampton, the lord William of Montagu, earl of Sarum, the lord Hugh of Audley, earl of Gloucester, the lord William of Clinton, earl of Huntingdon, the lord Robert of Ufford, earl of Suffolk. These creations were made in the second Sunday in Lent, at Westminster; where also he made 24 knights. Also in the same parliament it was enacted that no wool growing in England should leave the realm, but that cloth should be made with it in England, and that all makers of cloth should be welcomed in England wherever they might come from, and that fit places should be assigned to them and that they should have wages from the king until they could make fitting gain by their craft. Also it was enacted that no one should use cloth made outside England and afterwards imported, except the king and queen and their children. From which statutes no results followed, nor did any one take the trouble to observe them.

(Yet the Flemish weavers, who were entirely dependent upon England for their wool, were thereby reduced to great distress.)

1329-1333.—How the lord sir Robert of Artois was chased out of the realm of France.

Froissart, ch. 25 (I. § 48).   *Jehan le Bel*, ch. 19.

The man in the world that most aided king Philip to attain to the crown of France was sir Robert, earl of Artois, who was one of the sagest

and greatest lords in France, and come of high
lineage from the blood royal, and had to his wife
the sister of the said king Philip, and always was
his chief and special companion and lover in all his
estates. And the space of three years all that was
done in the realm of France was done by his advice,
and without him nothing was done. And, after, it
fortuned that this king Philip took a marvellous
great displeasure and hatred against this noble man,
sir Robert of Artois, for a plea that was moved
before him whereof the earl of Artois was
cause. For he would fain have won his intent by
virtue of a letter that he laid forth, the which was
not true as it was said. Wherefore the king was in
such displeasure that if he had taken him in his ire
surely it had cost him his life, without remedy. So
this sir Robert was fain to fly the realm of France,
and went to Namur to the earl John, his nephew.
Then the King took the earl's wife and her two
sons, who were his own nephews, John and Charles,
and did put them in prison. And they were kept
straitly, and the king swear that they should never
come out of prison as long as they lived; the king's
mind would be turned by no manner of means.

(Robert of Artois came to England probably in 1334, and in
1337 Edward gave him certain estates and a pension.)

1337.—How king Edward was counselled to make war against the French king.

Froissart, ch. 28 (I. § 56).   *Jehan le Bel*, ch. 25.

In this season when this crusade was in great

forwardness, for there was no speaking but thereof, sir Robert of Artois was as then in England, banished out of France, and was ever about king Edward; and always he counselled him to defy the French king, who kept his heritages from him wrongfully; of which matter the king oftentimes counselled with them of his secret council, for gladly he would have had his right if he wist how. And also he thought that if he should demand his right and it were refused, what he might do then to amend it. For if he should then sit still and do not his devoir to recover his right, he should be more blamed than before; yet he thought it were better to speak not thereof. For he saw well that by the puissance of his realm it would be hard for him to subdue the great realm of France without help from some other great lords, either of the empire or in other places, for his money. The king oftentimes desired counsel of his chief and special friends and counsellors. Finally, his counsellors answered him and said, "Sir, the matter is so weighty and of so high an enterprise that we dare not speak therein nor give you any counsel. But, sir, this we would counsel you to do: send sufficient messengers, well informed of your intention, to the earl of Hainault, whose daughter you have married, and to sir John of Hainault, his brother, who hath valiantly served you at all times. And desire them, by way of love, that they would counsel you in this matter, for they know better what pertaineth to such a matter than we do.

And, sir, if they agree to your intent, then will they counsel you what friends you may best make." The king was content with this answer, and desired the bishop of Lincoln to take on him this message, and with him two bannerets and two doctors. They made them ready and took shipping and arrived at Dunkirk, and rode through Flanders till they came to Valenciennes, where they found the earl lying in his bed sick of the gout, and with him sir John his brother. They were greatly feasted, and declared the cause of their coming, and showed all the reasons and doubts that the king their master had made. Then the earl said: "So help me God, if the king's mind might be brought to pass, I would be right glad thereof; for I had rather the wealth of him that hath married my daughter, than of him that never did nothing for me, though I have married his sister. And also he did hinder the marriage of the young duke of Brabant who should have married one of my daughters. Wherefore I shall not fail to aid my dear and well beloved son, the king of England. I shall give him counsel and aid to the best of my power, and so shall do John my brother who hath served him ere this. Howbeit he must have more help than ours, for Hainault is but a small country in regard to the realm of France, and England is far off to aid us." Then the bishop said, "Sir, we thank you in our master's behalf, for the comfort that you give us. Sir, we desire you to give our master counsel what friends he were best to labour unto to aid him." "Surely," said the earl, "I can not devise a more puissant prince to aid him than the duke of Brabant who is his cousin germain. And also the bishop of Liège, the duke of Gueldres, who hath his sister to his wife, the archbishop of Cologne, the marquis of Juliers, sir Arnold of Blenkenheim, and the lord of Falkenberg. These lords are they that may make most men of war in a short space of any that I know. They are good men of war; they may well make ten thousand men of war so they have wages thereafter; they are people that would gladly win advantage. If it were so that the king, my son, your master, might get these lords to be on his part, and so to come into these parts, he might well go over the water of Oise and seek out king Philip to fight with him." With this answer these ambassadors returned into England to the king and reported all that they had done, whereof the king had great joy and was well comforted.*

1337.—To explain to the people the promises made to the king of France in order to preserve peace.

Rymer. Fœdera, 994.

(In this manifesto before beginning the war with France, Edward does not claim the French crown, and complains only of Philip's action in Guienne and Scotland.)

The king to the venerable father in Christ, John, archbishop of Canterbury, primate of all England, and to his trusty and well-beloved William of Clin-

---

* For Edward's claim to the French crown, see *Appendix*.

ton, earl of Huntingdon, who have been appointed to declare in the county of Kent certain things touching the defence of our realm, of holy church, and of our other lands, greeting;

We send you a certain schedule, herein enclosed, of the promises which we and our ambassadors have made to prevent war with the king of France;

Commanding you, and each of you, that you cause what is contained in that schedule to be clearly and fully explained to the clergy and people of that county, on the day and at the place mentioned in the commission which has been issued to you;

Persuading them, by all the ways and means you can, since that king threatens us with war, willing to consent neither to peace nor to negotiations for peace, whereby we are subjected to intolerable expense for public defence, to help us freely each of them, as far as their means permit; so acting in this, that we may have to justly commend your diligence.

Witness the king, at Westminster, the 28th day of August. By the king.

A similar order was sent to the following persons appointed in the following counties to make the same announcement—

(Then follows a list of persons so appointed, *e.g.*, in Oxfordshire and Bucks., the abbots of Abingdon and Osney and three knights.)

Schedule mentioned in the above order.

These are the offers made to the king of France by the king of England to prevent war.

In the first place, the king of England sent to the king of France divers solemn messages, praying him to restore the lands that he withheld from him, wilfully and against reason, in the duchy of Guienne; to none of which requests did the king of France consent; but at last he promised that, if the king of England would come to him in person, he would shew him justice, grace, and favour.

Trusting to this promise, the king of England passed privately into France and went to him, humbly requesting the return of those lands, offering and performing to the king what he was bound to do and more; but the king of France gave him words only and not deeds, and, moreover, while the negotiations were going on, encroached wrongfully more and more on the rights of the king of England in that duchy.

Also the king of England, seeing the harshness of the king of France, in order to have his good will and that which he wrongfully kept from him, made him the great offers below mentioned; that is to say, when one was refused he made him another;

First, the marriage of his eldest son, now duke of Cornwall, with the daughter of the king of France, without dowry;

Then, the marriage of his sister, now countess of Gueldres, with his son, with a very great sum of money;

Then, the marriage of his brother, the earl of

Cornwall, whom God assoil, with any lady of the blood royal of France;

Then, to make redemption for disturbance, he offered him as much money as he could reasonably demand;

Then, since the king of France gave the king of England to understand, that he wished to undertake a crusade to the Holy Land, and greatly desired to have the company of the king of England, and that he would do him grace and favour therefor, the king of England, in order that the prevention of the crusade might not be attributed to him, offered to the king of France to go in force with him on the crusade; provided, however, that before going, he made full restitution to him of his lands;

Then, he offered to go with him on crusade, on condition that he made restitution of half or a certain part of his lands;

Then, afterwards, he offered, with still greater liberality, to go with him on condition that, on his return from the Holy Land, he made full restitution.

Then, to stay the malice of the king of France, who tried to put upon the king of England the blame of preventing the crusade, he declared himself ready to undertake the crusade, on condition that, on his return, he did him justice.

But the king of France, who endeavoured in all ways that he could to injure the king of England and all his subjects, that he might keep what he unjustly withheld and conquer more from him, would not accept any of these offers, but seeking occasion to injure him, gave aid and maintenance to the Scots, the enemies of the king of England, trying to prevent him, by the Scotch war, from seeking his rights elsewhere.

Also, then, from respect to the king of France and at his request, the king of England granted to the Scots a cessation of the war and a truce, with hope of bringing about the peace;

But, during the truce, the Scots killed the earl of Athol and others, and took many nobles faithful to the king of England, and besieged and took castles and other places from the king and his subjects;

And, recently, at his request, he offered to the Scots a truce for four or five years, on condition that they restored what they had taken during the former truce, in order that the crusade might take place in the meantime;

To which restoration the king of France would not consent, but supported the Scots in their malice with all his power, and made open war without just cause on the king of England, and sent to sea his galleys and navy which he had prepared under pretence of the crusade, with a great number of armed men, to destroy the navy and subjects of the king of England;

Which men have taken in war and spoiled many ships of England and killed and taken the men who were in them, and have landed in England and the islands of the king of England, committing arson, homicide, robberies, and other horrible crimes, according to their power.

Also then the king of England by the counsel and advice of the magnates and wise men of the realm, wishing to prevent the war if possible, sent solemn messages to the king of France, to offer him all he could without great disherison, to obtain peace ;

But the king of France, hardened in his malice, would not suffer these messages to be brought to him, nor consent to peace or negotiations for peace ; but sent a great and strong army to take into his hands by force the duchy before mentioned ; declaring, untruly, that the duchy was forfeited ;

Which army did great evils in the duchy, besieging and taking castles and towns as far as they could.

Also the king of France, to cover his malice, did try to misinform the pope and the other great men of Christendom with regard to the king of England ; aiming at conquering, as far he can, not only that duchy, but all the lands of the king of England.

These proposals and others the king of England and his council could think of, have been made to the king of France to secure peace, and if any man can find any other fitting way, he will be bound and ready to accept it.

1337. — How Jacques d'Artevelde governed all Flanders.

Froissart, ch. 29 (I. § 59). *Jehan le Bel,* ch. 25.

(The immediate cause of the rising in Ghent was the wool-famine, due to the count's hostility to England. The aristocratic canon of Liège, Jehan le Bel, is strongly prejudiced against the popular leader, and thus the following account is full of misrepresentation.)

In this season there was great discord between the earl of Flanders and the Flemings, for they would not obey him; and he durst not abide in Flanders but in great peril. And in the town of Ghent there was a man, a maker of honey, called Jacques d'Artevelde. He was entered into such fortune and grace of the people that all things were done that he did devise; he might command what he would through all Flanders, for there was no man, though he were never so great, that durst disobey his commandment. He had always going with him up and down in Ghent sixty or four score varlets armed, and among them there were three or four that knew the secrets of his mind. So that if he met a person that he hated or had in suspicion, immediately he was slain. For he had commanded his secret varlets that wheresoever he met any person and made such a sign to them, that immediately they should slay him whatsoever he were, without any words or reasoning. And by that means he made many to be slain, whereby he was so dreaded that none durst speak against anything that he willed to be done; so that every man was glad to make him good cheer. And these varlets when they had brought him home to his house, then they should go to dinner where they list; and after dinner return again into the street before his lodging, and there abide till he come out and to wait on him till supper time. These soldiers had each of them four Flemish groats by the day, and were paid truly weekly. Thus he had in every town soldiers and servants at his wages ready to do his commandment, and to espy if there were any person that would rebel against his mind, and to inform him thereof. And as soon as he knew any such he would never cease till they were banished or slain without respite. All such great men, as knights, squires, or burgesses of good towns, as he thought favourable to the earl in any manner, he banished them out of Flanders; and he would levy the moiety of their lands to his own use, and leave the other half to their wives and children. Such as were banished, of whom there were a great number, abode at Saint Omer. To speak properly, there was never in Flanders, nor in none other country, prince, duke, nor other, that ruled a country so peaceably, so long as this Jacques d'Artevelde did rule Flanders. He levied the rents, winages, and rights that pertained to the earl throughout all Flanders, and spent all at his pleasure without any account making. And when he would say that he lacked money they believed him, and so it behoved them to do, for none durst say against him. When he would borrow anything of any burgess, there was none durst say him nay.

Now the English Ambassadors kept an honourable estate at the town of Valenciennes. They thought it should be a great comfort to the king, their lord, if they might get the Flemings to take their part. Then they took counsel of the earl (of Hainault) in that matter and he answered that truly it should be one of the greatest aids that they could have. But he said he thought their labour could not prevail without they get first the goodwill of Jacques d'Artevelde. Then they said they would essay what they could do; and so, thereupon, they departed from Valenciennes and went into Flanders, and departed into three or four companies. Some went to Bruges, some to Ypres, and some to Ghent. And all kept such state and spent so much that it seemed that silver and gold fell out of their hands; and they made many great promises and offers to them that they spake to for that matter. And the bishop, with a certain man with him, went to Ghent, and he did so much, what with fair words and otherwise, that he got the accord of Jaques d'Artevelde. And he got great grace in the town, and specially of an old knight that dwelt in Ghent, who was there right well beloved, called the lord of Courtraisen, a knight banneret, reputed for a hardy knight, who had always served truly his lords. This knight did much honour to the Englishmen, as a valiant knight ought to do to all strangers. Of this he was accused to the French king, who immediately sent a strait commandment to the earl of Flanders that he should send for this said knight, and as soon as he had him to strike off his head. The earl, who durst not break the King's commandment, did so much that this knight came to him

at his sending as one that thought no evil, and at
once he was taken and his head struck off; whereof
many folks were sorry and were sore displeased with
the Count, for he was well beloved with the lords
of the country. These English lords did so much
that Jacques d'Artevelde divers times had together
the councils of the good towns to speak of the
business that these lords of England desired, and
of the franchises and amities that they offered them
in the king of England's behalf. So often they
spake of this matter, that finally they agreed that
the king of England might come and go into
Flanders at his pleasure. Howbeit, they said they
were so sore bound to the French king that they
might not enter into the realm of France to make
any war.

1337, Nov. 11.—Of the battle of Cadsand between the Englishmen and the Frenchmen.

Froissart, ch. 30-1 (I. § 63).

(Although no formal declaration of war between Edward and
Philip of Valois had yet been made, the French fleet attacked
Portsmouth, and the English attacked Cadsand.)

In this season there were in the isle of Cadsand
certain knights and squires of Flanders in garrison.
. . . They kept that passage against the Englishmen and made covert war. And when Edward heard
of the garrison of Cadsand, he said he would provide
for them shortly. And anon after, he ordained the
earl of Derby, sir Walter Manny, and divers other
knights and squires with five hundred men of arms

and two thousand archers, and they took shipping at London in the river Thames. The first tide they went to Gravesend, the next day to Margate, and at the third tide they took the sea and sailed into Flanders. So they apparelled themselves and came near to Cadsand.

When the Englishmen saw the town of Cadsand before them, they made them ready, and had wind and tide to serve them. And so in the name of God and Saint George they approached, and blew up their trumpets, and set their archers before them, and sailed toward the town. They of Cadsand saw well this great ship approach. They knew well they were Englishmen, and arranged themselves on the dykes and on the sands with their banners before them; and they made sixteen new knights. They were five thousand men of war, good knights and squires. There was sir Guy of Flanders, a good and a sure knight, but he was a bastard, and he desired all his company to do well their devoir. The Englishmen were desirous to assail and the Flemings to defend. The English archers began to shout and cried their cries, so that such as kept the passage were fain perforce to recoil back. At this first assault there were divers sore hurt, and the Englishmen took land and came and fought hand to hand. The Flemings fought valiantly to defend the passage, and the Englishmen assaulted chivalrously. The earl of Derby was that day a good knight; and at the first assault he was so forward that he was striken to the earth. And then

the lord of Manny did him great comfort, for by
pure feat of arms he raised him up again and brought
him out of peril, and cried, "Lancaster! for the earl
of Derby!" Then they approached on every part
and many were hurt, but more of the Flemings than
the Englishmen, for the archers shot so wholly
together that they did the Flemings much damage.
Thus in the haven of Cadsand there was a sore
battle; for the Flemings were good men of war,
chosen out by the earl of Flanders to defend
that passage against the Englishmen. . . . . .

There was a sore battle and well fought, hand
to hand, but finally the Flemings were put to the
chase and were slain more than three thousand,
what in the haven, streets, and houses. Sir Guy,
the bastard of Flanders, was taken, and sir Dutres
of Hallwyn and sir John of Rhodes were slain,
and the two brethren of Bonquedent, and sir Giles
de L'Etriefe, and more than twenty-six knights and
squires. And the town was taken, pillaged, and
all the goods and prisoners put into the ships and
the town burnt. And so thus the Englishmen
returned into England without any damage. The
King caused sir Guy, bastard of Flanders, to swear
and to bind himself prisoner. And in the same
year he became English, and did faith and homage
to the King of England.

1338.—How Black Agnes defended Dunbar.

Chronicle of Lanercost, 295-298.

(The siege of Dunbar was the last great effort of Edward

in Scotland; after five months it had to be abandoned, and Edward henceforth directed his efforts chiefly against France).

The king sent the lord William of Montague, earl of Salisbury, the earl of Gloucester, the earl of Derby, three barons, Percy, Neville, and Stafford, and the earl of Riddesdale, with twenty thousand men, into Scotland, to join the Scotch king (Balliol), ordering them vigorously to besiege the castle of Dunbar, which annoyed and troubled the whole land of Lothian. So the castle was besieged without intermission, and those within were surrounded with a deep ditch that they should not escape, and wooden houses were made in front of the gate, and tents were erected in which the more noble of the army dwelt. . . . . . But the castle defended itself manfully; for the countess of March, who was the chief warden of the castle, was the sister of the earl of Moray, who had been taken prisoner in Scotland and taken to England to the castle of Nottingham and there imprisoned. . . . . . After Easter, this earl was taken back to Scotland to Dunbar, to see if the countess, his sister, would give up the castle to save his life; but she replied that it was her lord's castle and given her to guard, nor would she yield it to any save at his command; and when those who were besieging her said that then her brother should die, she replied, "If you do that, then I shall be heir of the earldom of Moray," for her brother had no children. However, the English did not like to do what they had threatened, but preferred to take him back to Eng-

land and keep him in prison, as before. . . . .
And then because the king wished to cross the sea,
the lord William of Montague and the other earls
who were with him at the siege of Dunbar, unwilling
that he should go to any peril without them, gave
truce to those who were in the castle, on condition
that during the truce no change should be made
around or within the castle, or in the houses that
the English had made outside, although this could
not afterwards be observed.

(The Scotch rhyming chronicler, Andrew of Wyntown, tells
how Montague had made
"a mickel and right stalwart engine,"
and "warped * at the walls great stones,"
but all in vain,
" And also when they casten had,
With a towel a damosel
Arrayëd jolily † and well
Wipëd the wall that they might see
To make them more annoyed be." ll. 4859, sqq.)

1338.—How Edward crossed the sea and was made Vicar of the Empire.

Knighton, 2571-2.

Then was made a truce between England and
Scotland to last for one year, and the siege of
Dunbar was raised. King Edward meanwhile sent
beyond sea the lord William Bohun, earl of Northampton, and the lord Geoffrey Scrope the chief
justice of England and many others who landed at
Antwerp in Brabant. On the day of the Translation

* Threw.   † Prettily.

of S. Thomas, when all had been arranged and provided for the passage, the king put to sea with a great force, having with him the earls and magnates of the realm, such as the earls of Derby, of Salisbury, and Norfolk, and many nobles with them, and a great multitude of archers and Welsh: and he landed at Antwerp to join his wife and sons, on the feast of S. Kenelm. The Flemings rejoiced at his arrival and promised their aid: for he had given them satisfaction in the matter of certain ships that the English had taken from them and destroyed. . . . . . And when the king had come into those parts he found none in whom he could trust, so that he told the bishop of Lincoln and his other councillors that he had been ill advised. With headstrong course he pursued his way for eight days to Cologne to the duke of Bavaria, who had made himself emperor and dwelt in High Germany.* When the emperor heard of the coming of king Edward, he came to meet him, journeying for four days to a certain town of the name of Coblenz, and there he received the king with great honour. One chair was prepared for the emperor, one for the king, richly decked in the market place out-of-doors; there sat the emperor and king Edward beside him; and there were with them four dukes, three archbishops, and six bishops, and thirty-seven earls, and of barons, bannerets, knights, and other comers according to the reckoning of the heralds seventeen thousand. The emperor held in his right hand the imperial sceptre, and in his left

* See *Appendix*.

hand a round gold ball, which signifies the rule of the whole world; while over his head a knight held an unsheathed sword. There in the presence of the assembled people the emperor declared the unnaturalness, disobedience, and depravity that the king of France had shewn towards him; defied the king of France; and declared him and all his adherents under forfeiture. Then the emperor made king Edward his vicar, and gave him full power in his stead from Cologne to the sea; and in addition gave him a charter in the sight of all the people. On the morrow there came together at the mother-church the emperor and the king of England with the rest of the magnates and the archbishops, and they celebrated mass, and immediately after mass both the emperor and all the other magnates swore that they would help and support him against the king of France, to live and to die, for the next seven years following, supposing that war between the said kings should last so long. And likewise they all swore to the king of England that all the princes from Cologne to the sea would speedily join the king of England, and be always ready to march at any time that they were summoned, against the king of France, either in his company or when he should appoint. And if it should happen that any of them did not obey the king of England in the foregoing, all the other princes of high Germany would rise against him and destroy him. These treaties having been made, the king took leave of the emperor and returned to Brabant.

1339.—How the king of England and the French king appointed a day to fight together.

Froissart, ch. 40-2 (I. §§ 84-88).

(The greater part of the year was occupied with negotiations with the German princes and with the pope, who urged Edward to dissolve his alliance with the excommunicated emperor, Louis of Bavaria. In the autumn, the king brought together his allies, and made his first attempt on France, crossing the Oise, and meeting the French army near S. Quentin.)

Thus these two kings were lodged between Buironfosse and Flamengery in the plain fields without any advantage. I think there was never seen before so goodly an assembly of noble men together, as was there. When the king of England, being in the chapel of Tierache, knew how that king Philip was within two leagues, then he called the lords of his host together, and demanded of them what he should do, his honour saved, for he said that his intention was to give battle. Then the lords beheld each other, and they desired the duke of Brabant to show first his intent; the duke said, that he agreed that they should give battle, for otherwise, he said, they could not depart saving their honours; wherefore he counselled that they should send heralds to the French king to demand a day of battle. Then a herald of the duke of Gueldres, who knew well the language of French, was informed what he should say and so he rode till he came into the French host; and then he drew him to king Philip and to his council, and said: "Sir, the king of England is in the field and desireth to have battle, power against power"; the which thing king Philip granted and took the day, the Friday next after; and then it was Wednesday. And so the herald returned, well rewarded with good furred gowns given him by the French king and other lords because of the tidings that he brought. So thus the day was agreed upon, and knowledge was made thereof to all the lords of both the hosts, and so every man made him ready to the matter. The Thursday in the morning there were two knights of the earl of Hainault's, the lord Faguinelles and the lord of Tupeney, they mounted on their horses, and they two all alone departed from the French host, and rode to view the English host; so they rode coasting the host, and it fortuned that the lord of Faguinelles' horse took the bridle in the teeth in such wise that his master could not rule him; and so, whether he would or not, the horse brought him into the English host, and there he fell in the hands of the Germans, who perceived well that he was none of their company, and set on him, and took him and his horse; and so he was prisoner to five or six gentlemen of Germany; and anon they set him to his ransom. And when they understood that he was a Hainaulter, they demanded of him if he knew sir John of Hainault, and he answered "Yes" and desired them for the love of God to bring him to his presence, for he knew well that he would pay his ransom for him; thereof were the Germans joyous, and so brought him to the lord Beaumont, who immediately did pledge him out from his masters' hands; and the lord of Faguinelles returned again to the earl of Hainault, and he had his horse again delivered to him at the request of the lord Beaumont. Thus passed that day, and none other thing done that ought to be remembered.

When the Friday came, in the morning both hosts apparelled themselves ready, and every lord heard mass among their own companies, and divers were shriven. . . . . . It might well be marvelled, how so goodly a sight of men of war so near together should depart without battle. But the Frenchmen were not all of one accord; they were of divers opinions; some said it were a great shame an they fought not, seeing their enemies so near them in their own country, ranged in the field, and also had promised to fight with them; and some other said it should be a great folly to fight, for it was hard to know every man's mind, and jeopardy of treason: for, they said, if fortune were contrary to their king, as to lose the field, he then should put his whole realm in a jeopardy to be lost; and even if he did discomfort his enemies, yet, for all that, he should be never the nearer of the realm of England, nor of such lands pertaining to any of those lords that be with him allied. Thus in striving of divers opinions the day passed, till it was past noon; and then suddenly there started a hare among the Frenchmen; and such as saw her cried and made great noise, whereby such as were behind thought they before had been fighting, and so put on their helms and took their spears in their hands, and so there were made divers new knights, and especially the earl of Hainault made thirteen, who were ever after called knights of the hare. Thus that battle stood still all that Friday; and besides this strife between the councillors of France, there were brought in letters to the host of recommendation to the French king and to his council from king Robert of Sicily, the which king, as it was said, was a great astronomer, and full of great science. He had often times sought his books on the estate of the kings of England and of France, and he found by his astrology and by the influence of the heavens, that if the French king ever fought with king Edward of England, he should be discomforted; wherefore he, like a king of great wisdom and as he that doubted the peril of the French king his cousin, sent often times letters to king Philip and to his council, that in no wise he should make any battle against the Englishmen, where king Edward was personally present. So that, what with doubt and with such writing from the king of Sicily, divers of the great lords of France were sore abashed; and also king Philip was informed thereof. Howbeit, yet he had great will to give battle; but he was so counselled to the contrary, that the day passed without battle and every man withdrew to their lodgings. And when the earl of Hainault saw that they would not fight he departed with all his whole company, and went back the same night to Quesnoy. And the king of England, the duke of Brabant, and all the other lords retired, and trussed all their baggages and went the same night to Davesnes, in Hainault.

And the next day they took leave each of other; and the Germans and the Brabanters departed, and the king went into Brabant with the duke his cousin.

1340, Jan.—How king Edward took on him to bear the arms of France, and the name to be called king thereof.

Froissart, ch. 43 (I. §§ 88-90).   *Jehan le Bel*, ch. 33.

Then the king of England was sore desired of all his allies in the empire that he should require them of Flanders to aid and to maintain his war, and to defy the French king, and to go with him where he would have them; and that, on their so doing, he should promise them to recover Lille, Douay, and Bethune.* This request was well heard of the Flemings, and thereupon they desired to take counsel among themselves. And so they took counsel at good leisure, and then they said to the king, "Sir, ere this time ye have made to us request in this behalf. Sir, if we might well do this, saving your honour, and to save ourselves, we would gladly do it. But, sir, we be bound by faith and oath, and on the sum of two million florins in the pope's chamber, that we may make or move no war against the king of France, on pain to lose the said sum and beside that to run in danger of the sentence of cursing. But, sir, if you will take on you the arms of France and quarter them with the arms of England, and call yourself king

* Yielded to the king of France by the "Iniquitous Treaty" of 1305.

of France, as you ought to be of right, then we will take you for rightful king of France and demand of you quittance of our bonds; and so you will give us pardon thereof, as king of France. By this means we shall be assured and acquitted withal, and so then we will go with you whithersoever you will have us." Then the king took counsel, for he thought it was a sore matter to take on him the arms of France and the name, while, as then, he had conquered nothing thereof, nor could not tell what should fall thereof nor whether he should conquer it or not. And, on the other side, loth he was to refuse the comfort and aid of the Flemings, who might do him more aid than any other. So the king took counsel of the lords of the empire and of the lord Robert of Artois, and with other of his special friends, and so that finally, the good and the evil weighed, he answered to the Flemings, that if they would swear and seal to this agreement, and promise to maintain his war, he would do all this with a good will, and promised to get them again Lille, Douay, and Bethune. And they all answered that they were content. Then there was a day assigned to meet at Ghent, at the which day the King was there, and the most part of the said lords, and all the councils generally in Flanders. And so then all these said matters were rehearsed, sworn, and sealed; and the king quartered the arms of France with England, and from thenceforth took on him the name of the king of France and so continued till he left it again by composition.

Thus every man departed and went home. The king of England went to Antwerp, and the queen abode still at Ghent, and was oftentimes visited by Jacques d'Artevelde and by other lords, ladies, and damsels of Ghent.

(Next month Edward returned to England.)

1339.—At a College Meeting.

Rogers, History of Agriculture, ii. 672.

(At Merton College, Oxford, the warden and fellows were bound to meet three times a year at a "scrutiny," wherein each gave his opinion on the condition of the college. Of three of these meetings some rough notes, taken by one who was present, have been preserved.)

Middleton.—William the chaplain has often insulted the fellows.

Handel.—It would be well if the senior fellows were summoned to make peace between Wylie and Finmer.

Westcombe.—The noise the fellows make in their rooms.

Humberstone.—The quarrel between Wylie and Finmer. The fellows keep dogs, and progress in their studies is prevented by idleness. The statute is not observed, for we have no bursars. Also it would be well if the land in Little Wolford were let to a farmer.

Finmer.—Wylie, although appointed under the statute to audit accounts, will not audit them, and though thrice summoned and again called upon by the fellows, has rebelliously refused, and so falls under the statute ; and he unjustly receives better commons, and they who ought to proceed against him are too remiss.

Wanting.—The warden should not go on insulting the senior fellows in the way he has begun.

Hylie.—Somebody should be sent to Stratton to enquire about the college estates and other business.

Lynham.—As to allaying the quarrels among the fellows.

Sutton.—They ought to have a keeper of pledges,* but have not, and there is a deficit ; and it is said that some books are sold, without the college or the fellows benefiting by it. The warden does not enforce process against the debtors of the college and especially against the bailiff of Elham ; and Wanting owes the bailiff of Elham seven pounds and sixteen pence which belong to the college, and as he excuses himself from all other business, he ought not to take a part in these college meetings. . . . .

Handel would be glad if a volume of decrees and of decretals were placed in the library and if the books of the college were arranged. .

Buckingham.—Wanting has sold the college horses at Elham, and has kept the money in his hands, and has rendered no account nor has the bailiff. . . . There should not be a number of people taking notes in the meeting.

* Deposited with the college by students to whom loans had been made.

Dumbleton.—Nothing.

Monby.—Wylie has publicly, in the presence of all the fellows, insulted Finmer.

Leverington.—The seneschal is not present in chapel on saints' days, but is absent for the most part.

. . . .

Wylie begs that what has been said by Elyndon and Wanting be corrected, and recommends charity. The warden should correct it, especially what had been said to the warden in the meeting, and above all what Elyndon said, that the reputations of some of the fellows were tarnished; and how that Durant accused Wylie of planning with the other seniors to prevent the election of a fellow, and that he had this from those who were recently in London.

Middleton.—Elham is in fault as to the breaking of the hall door. We ought to have a mill at Seaton.

Handel.—This opportunity should be taken of restoring peace. The juniors should show reverence to the seniors, and everyone should be enjoined publicly to observe charity, and each should try to bring this about as far as he can.

Humberstone.—The warden ought by statute to get the help of some of the fellows who are impartial to put an end to the quarrel between Wylie and Finmer. Wanting has behaved disrespectfully towards the warden by publicly addressing him as Robert.

1340.—A Lesson on Usury.

Ayenbite of Inwyt (Remorse of Conscience), ed. Early English Text Society, p. 35.

(The two following extracts are most valuable illustrations of the teaching of the pulpit and confessional. The *direct* payment of interest was illegal.)

There are seven kinds of usury. The first is lending that lendeth silver for other things, where over and above the capital sum the lender taketh the profits either in pence, or in horses, or in corn, or in wine, or in fruits of the ground that he taketh in mortgage, without reckoning these profits as part-payment. And what is worse, he will reckon twice, or even thrice in the year in order to raise the rate of usury, and yet he hath gifts as well for each term; and he maketh often of the usury a principal debt. These are usuries evil and foul. The courteous lender is he that lendeth without always making bargains for profit, either in pence, or in horses, or in cups of gold, or in silver, or in robes, or in tuns of wine, or in fat swine, or in services of horses or carts, or providings for himself or his children, or in any other things that he takes by reason of the loan. This is the first manner of usury, that is, lending wickedly. The other manner of usury is in those that do not themselves lend, but that which their fathers or the fathers of their wives or their elders have received in pledge and they inherit, by usury they retain and will not yield it up. The third manner of usury is in them that have shame to lend with their own hand, but they lend their pence through their servants or other men. These are the master money-lenders. Of such sin great men are not quit, who hold and sustain Jews and usurers that lend and destroy the country; and the great men take the rewards and the great gifts, and oftentimes the ransom-money of the goods of the poor. The fourth manner is in those that lend with other men's silver that they buy at small cost in order to lend at a greater. These are the little usurers that teach so much foul craft. The fifth manner is in bargaining when men sell a thing, whatsoever it is, for more than it is worth at the time. And what is worse, is wickedly selling at that time when they see their wares are most needed; then they sell the thing for twice the dearer, or thrice as much as the thing is worth. Such folk do much evil. For their bargaining destroyeth and maketh beggars of knights and nobles that follow tournaments. And they take their lands and their heritage in pledge and mortgage, from which they never acquit them. Others sin in buying things, as corn, or wine, or other things, for less than half the pence that it is worth, and then they sell them again for twice as much, or thrice the dearer. Others buy things when they are least worth and of great cheapness, as corn sold in harvest time, or wine, or bargains, in order to sell them again whenever they are most dear. And they wish for a dear time in order to sell the dearer. Others buy corn in the blade and vines in the flower, when they are of fair-shewing and good forwardness, that they may have, whatever befal, their wealth safe. The sixth manner is when they give their pence to merchants in such wise that they are fellows in winning but not in losing. . . . . . The seventh manner is in those that lend their poor neighbours, in their needs, a little silver, or corn, or do them a little courtesy. And when they see them poor and needy, then they make with them a bargain to do their work, and for the pence they have before given to the poor man or the corn they have lent him, they have three pennyworth of work for one penny.

1340.—A Lesson on Trade.
Ayenbite of Inwyt, ed. E.E.T.S., p. 44.

The eighth bough of Avarice is chaffering, wherein one sinneth in many ways, for worldly winning; and, namely, in seven manners. The first is to sell the things as dear as one may, and to buy as good cheap as one may. The next is lying, swearing, and forswearing, the higher to sell their wares. The third manner is by weights and measures, and that may be in three ways. The first when one hath divers weights or divers measures, and buyeth by the greatest weights or the greatest measures and selleth by the least. The other manner is when one hath rightful weights and rightful measures to sell untruly, as do the taverners that fill the measure with scum. The third manner is when those that sell by weight contrive that the thing that they weigh showeth more heavy. The fourth manner to sin in chaffering is to sell to time. Of this we have spoken above. The fifth manner is to sell otherwise than one hath showed before; as doth these scriveners that showeth good letter at beginning and after do badly. The sixth is to hide the truth about the thing that one will sell; as do the dealers of horses. The seventh is to contrive that the thing one selleth maketh for to show better than it is; as do the sellers of cloth that choose dim places wherein to sell their cloth. In many other manners one may sin in chafferings, but long thing it were to say.

1340.—Here beginneth the statute made at Westminster in the 14th year of king Edward the third.

Public General Acts, Anno xiv. Ed. III.

(In order to obtain supplies for the war, Edward gave his assent to several reforming statutes, of which the following is the most important. It is a clearer declaration than any previously made of the principle that no taxation should be imposed except by the consent of parliament.)

Edward by the grace of God, etc., to all them etc., greeting. Know ye that whereas the prelates, earls, barons, and commons of the realm of England, in our present parliament holden at Westminster, the Wednesday next after the Sunday of middle Lent, the 14th year of our reign of England and the first of France, have granted to us of their good grace and good will, in aid of the speed of our great business which we have to do as well on this side the sea as beyond, the 9th sheaf, the 9th fleece, and the 9th lamb to be taken by two years next coming . . . . and the citizens and burgesses of boroughs the true 9th part of all their goods, and merchants who dwell not in cities and boroughs as well as others who dwell in forests and wastes and live not of gain nor of store of sheep, the 15th of their goods lawfully to the value; we, willing to provide to the indemnity of the said prelates, earls, barons, and other of the commonalty, and also of the citizens, burgesses, and merchants aforesaid, will and grant for us and our heirs to the same prelates, earls, barons, and commons, citizens, burgesses, and merchants that the same grant which is so chargeable shall not another time be had forth in example nor fall to their prejudice in time to come, nor that they be from henceforth charged nor grieved to make any aid or to sustain charge, if it be not by the common assent of the prelates, earls, barons, and other great men and commons of the said realm of England and that in the parliament. And that all the profits rising of the said aid, and of wards and marriages, customs and escheats, and other profits rising of the said realm of England shall be set and dispended upon the maintenance of the safeguard of our said realm of England and of our wars of Scotland, France, and Gascony, and in no place elsewhere during the said wars.*

* For taxation under Edward the third, see *Appendix*.

1340, June 24.—Of the battle on the sea before Sluys in Flanders between the king of England and the Frenchmen.

Froissart, ch. 50 (I. § 114).

On midsummer even in the year of our Lord 1340, all the English fleet was departed out of the river of Thames, and took the way to Sluys. And the same time, between Blankenberg and Sluys on the sea, was sir Hugh Kiriel, sir Peter Bahucet, and Barbenoir, and more than sixscore great vessels besides others; and they were of Normans, Genoese, and Picards, about the number of forty thousand. There they were laid by the French king to bar the king of England's passage. The king of England and his men came sailing till they came before Sluys. And when the king saw so great a number of ships that their masts seemed to be like a great wood, he demanded of the master of his ship what people he thought they were. He answered and said, "Sir, I think they are Normans, laid here by the French king, and they have done great displeasure in England, burnt your town of Southampton and taken your great ship, the Christopher." "Ah!" quoth the king, "I have long desired to fight with the Frenchmen, and now shall I fight with some of them, by the grace of God and Saint George; for truly they have done me so many displeasures that I will be revenged, and I may." Then the king set all his ships in order, the greatest before, well furnished with archers, and ever between two ships of archers he had one ship with men of arms. Then he made another line to lie aloof with archers to comfort ever them that were most weary if need were. And there were a great number of countesses, ladies, knights' wives, and other damosels, that were going to see the queen at Ghent; these ladies the king caused to be well kept with three hundred men at arms and five hundred archers. When the king and his marshals had ordered his lines of battle, he drew up the sails and came with a quarter wind to have the advantage of the sun. And so, at last, they turned a little to get the wind at will; and when the Normans saw them recoil back they had marvel why they did so. And some said, "They think themselves not meet to meddle with us, wherefore they will go back." They saw well how the king of England was there personally, by reasons of his banners. Then they did put their fleet in order, for they were sage and good men of war on the sea; and did set the Christopher, the which they had won the year before, to be foremost, with many trumpets and instruments, and so set on their enemies. There began a sore battle on both parts; archers and crossbows began to shoot; men of arms approached and fought hand to hand; and the better to come together they had great hooks and grappling irons to cast out of one ship into another, and so tied them fast together. There were many deeds of arms done, taking and rescuing again. And at last the great Christopher was first won by the Englishmen, and all that were within it taken or slain. Then there was great noise and cry, and the Englishmen approached and fortified the Christopher with archers, and made it to pass on before to fight with the Genoese. This battle was right fierce and terrible, for the battles on the sea are more dangerous and fiercer than the battles by land; for on the sea there is no recoiling nor fleeing, there is no remedy but to fight and to abide fortune and every man to shew his prowess. Of a truth sir Hugh Kiriel and sir Bahucet and Barbenoir were right good and expert men of war. This battle lasted from the morning till it was noon and the Englishmen endured much pain, for their enemies were four against one and all good men on the sea. There the king of England was a noble knight of his own hands; he was in the flower of his youth. In likewise so were the earls of Derby, Pembroke, Hereford, Huntingdon, Northampton, and Gloucester, sir Reynold Cobham, sir Richard Stafford, the lord Percy, sir Walter of Manny, sir Henry of Flanders, sir John Chandos, sir Robert of Artois, called the earl of Richmond, and divers other lords and knights who bore themselves so valiantly, with some succours that they had of Bruges and of the country there about, that they obtained the victory. So that the Frenchmen, Normans, and others were discomfitted, slain, and drowned; there was not one that escaped, but all were slain. When this victory was achieved, the king all that night abode in his ship before Sluys with great noise of trumpets and other instruments. Thither came to see the king divers of Flanders, such as heard of the king's coming. And then

the king demanded of the burgesses of Bruges how
Jacques d'Artevelde did. They answered that he
was gone to the earl of Hainault against the duke
of Normandy with sixty thousand Flemings. And
the next day, the which was midsummer day, the
king and all his took land. And the king, on
foot, went a pilgrimage to our lady of Ardenburg
and there heard mass and dined; and then took
his horse and rode to Ghent, where the queen
received him with great joy; and all his baggage
came after, little by little. Then the king wrote
to the count of Hainault and to them within the
castle of Thun*, certifying them of his arrival. And
when the count knew thereof, and that the king
had discomfited the army on the sea, he dislodged,
and gave leave to all the soldiers to depart. And
he took with him to Valenciennes all the great lords
and there feasted them honourably, and especially
the duke of Brabant and Jacques d'Artevelde. And
there Jacques d'Artevelde, openly in the market
place, in the presence of all the lords and of all
such as would hear him, declared what right the
king of England had to the crown of France, and
also how puissant the three countries were of
Flanders, Hainault, and Brabant, surely joined in
one alliance. And he did so by his great wisdom
and pleasant words that all people that heard him
praised him much, and said how he had nobly
spoken and by great experience. And thus he was
greatly praised and it was said that he was well

* Which had been besieged by the French.

worthy to govern the county of Flanders. Then the lords departed and promised to meet again within eight days at Ghent, to see the king of England, and so they did. And the king feasted them honourably, and so did the queen, who was as then newly delivered of a son called John, who afterwards became duke of Lancaster by his marriage to the daughter of duke Henry of Lancaster.

1340.—How the king of England besieged the city of Tournay with great puissance.

Froissart, ch. 53, 54, 56, 57, 63.

When the time approached that the king and his allies should meet before Tournay, and that the corn began to ripen, he departed from Ghent with seven earls of his country, eight prelates, thirty-eight baronets, two hundred knights, four thousand men at arms, and nine thousand archers, beside footmen. All his host passed through the town of Oudenarde, and so passed the river Scheldt, and lodged before Tournay at the gate called St. Martin, the way towards Lisle and Douai. Then anon after came the duke of Brabant with more than twenty thousand men, knights, squires, and commoners, and he lodged at the bridge of Ayres by the river Scheldt between the abbey of St. Nicholas and the gate Valentinois. Next to him came the earl of Hainault with a goodly company of his country, with many of Holland and Zealand, and he was lodged between the king and the duke of Brabant. Then came Jacques d'Artevelde with more than sixty thousand Flemings, beside them of Ypres, Poperingue, Cassel, Bruges. Jacques d'Artevelde lodged at the gate of St. Fountain. The duke of Gueldres, the earl of Juliers, and all the Germans were lodged on the other side towards Hainault. Thus the city of Tournay was environed round about, and every host might resort each to the other, so that none could issue without spying. The siege enduring, they without were well provided with victuals and at a proper price; for it came to them from all parts.

Also the Flemings oftentimes assailed them of Tournay, and had made ships, belfries, and instruments of assault; so that every day lightly there was skirmishing and divers hurt of one and other. The Flemings took much pain to trouble them of Tournay; among other assaults there was one endured a whole day; there were many feats of arms done, for all the lords and knights that were at Tournay were thereat; for the assault was made in ships and vessels wrought with intent to break the barriers and the postern of the arch; but it was so well defended that the Flemings won nothing; there they lost a ship with some six score men, the which were drowned, and at night they withdrew sore troubled. . . . . . . And because the victuals within the city began to minish, the French lords within caused to leave the town all manner of poor people, such as were not furnished to abide the adventure of the siege; they were put out in the open day, and they passed through the duke of Brabant's host, who showed their grief; for he caused them to be safely brought to the French host at Arras, where the king lay; and there he made a great assembly of men of his own country and part out of the empire. Thither came to him the king of Bohemia, the duke of Lorraine, the earl of Bar, the bishops of Metz and Verdun, the earl of Montbeliard, sir John of Chalons, the earl of Geneva, the earl of Savoy, and the lord Lewis of Savoy his brother. All these lords came to serve the French king with all their powers. Also thither came the duke of Brittany, the duke of Burgundy, the duke of Bourbon, the earl of Alençon, the earl of Flanders, the earl of Forêt, the earl of Armagnac, the earl of Blois, sir Charles of Blois, the earl of Harcourt, the earl of Dammartin, the lord Coucy, and divers other lords and knights. And after came the king of Navarre with a goodly number of men of war out of the country in France that he held of the French king. Also there was the king of Scots with a certain number appointed to him.

When all these said lords were come to Arras to the French king, then he removed and came to a little river three leagues from Tournay; the water was deep, and round about full of marshes, so that no man could pass but by a little way, so narrow that two horses could not pass abreast; there the king lay, and passed not the river, for he durst not. The next day the hosts lay still; some of the lords counselled to make bridges to pass over the water at their ease; then there were men sent to view the passage, and when they had well viewed everything, they thought it was but a lost labour, and they showed the king how that there was no passage but at the bridge of Tressin. Thus the matter abode in the same case. The tidings anon spread abroad how the French king was lodged between the bridge of Tressin and the bridge of Bouvines, to the intent to fight with his enemies, so that all manner of people, such as desired honour, drew to the one part and to the other as they owed their service or favour. . . . . This siege endured a long season, the space of eleven weeks all but three days, and all that season the lady Jane of Valois, sister to the French king and mother of the earl of Hainault, toiled greatly to have a respite and a peace between the parties, so that they might depart without battle; and divers times she knelt at the feet of the French king in that behalf, and also made great labour to the lords of the empire, and especially to the duke of Brabant and to the duke of Juliers, who had her daughter in marriage, and also to sir John of Hainault; so much the good lady procured that it was granted that each party should send four sufficient persons to treat on some good way to accord the parties, and a truce for three days; those appointed should meet in a little chapel standing in the fields called Espléchin. At the day appointed these persons met and the good lady with them; of the French party there was Charles king of Bohemia, Charles earl of Alençon, brother to the French king, and the bishop of Liège, the earl of Flanders, and the earl of Armagnac; of the English party there was the duke of Brabant, the bishop of

Lincoln, the duke of Gueldres, the duke of Juliers, and sir John of Hainault; and when they were all met, they made each to other great salutations, and then entered into their treaty; and all that day they communed on divers ways of accord, and always the good lady of Valois was among them, desiring effectually all the parties that they would do their labour to make a peace; howbeit, the first day passed without anything doing, and so they returned and promised to meet again the next day; the which day they came together again in the same place and so fell again into their treaty; and so fell unto certain points agreeable, but it was then so late that they could not put it in writing that day; and the third day they met again, and so finally accorded on a truce to endure for a year between all parties and all their men; and also between them that were in Scotland, and all such as made war in Gascony, Poitou, and in Saintonge. . . . .
This truce forthwith was cried in both hosts, whereof the Brabanters were right glad, for they were sore weary with so long lying at the siege; so that the next day, as soon as it was daylight, ye should have seen tents taken down, chariots charged, and people removed so quick, that a man would have thought to have seen a new world. Thus the good town of Tournay was safe, without any great damage; howbeit, they within endured great pain; their victuals began to fail; for they had then scant to serve them, for three or four days at the

most. The king of England departed sore against his mind, if he might have done otherwise, but he was fain to follow the wills of the other lords and to believe their counsels. And the French king could abide no longer where he lay for the evil air and the hot weather, so the Frenchmen had the honour of that journey because they had rescued Tournay and caused their enemies to depart. The king of England and the lords on his party said how they had the honour by reason that they had tarried so long within the realm, and besieged one of the good towns thereof, and had also wasted and burned in the French country, and that the French king had not rescued it in time and hour, as he ought to have done by giving of battle, and had finally agreed to a truce, his enemies being still at the siege and burning his country. Thus these lords departed from the siege of Tournay, and every man drew to his own, and the king of England came to Ghent to the queen, his wife.

1340-1.—How the king returned to London and removed his ministers.

Murimuth, p. 109.

Afterwards when all the English who were with the king at Ghent, believed that the king of England would celebrate Christmas there, the king feigning he was going out for exercise, rode off secretly with only eight attendants, and scarcely telling any of his friends came to Zeeland, and went on board. He sailed for three days and nights and on the night of S. Andrew's, about cockcrow, entered the tower of

London by water; and with him were the earl of Northampton, the lord Walter of Manny, . . . and a few others. And immediately at cockcrow he sent for the chancellor, treasurer, and justices then present in London; and immediately removed the bishop of Chichester from the office of chancellor, and the bishop of Coventry from the office of treasurer, and he wished to send them into Flanders and put them in pledge there, or if they refused this, to keep them against their will in the tower of London. But the bishop of Chichester explained to him the danger which he incurred from the canon which threatens those who imprison bishops, and so he allowed them to leave the Tower. But the chief justices, namely the lord John of Stonor, the lord William of Willoughby, the lord William of Shereshull, and especially the lord Nicolas de la Beche who before was warden of the tower of London, as well as the merchants, the lord John of Pultenay, William de la Pole and Richard his brother, and the chief clerks of the chancery, namely the lords John of S. Paul, Michael of Wath, Henry of Stretford, Robert of Chikwelle, and of the treasury the lord Thomas of Thorpe and many others, he caused to be committed to divers prisons. But since this had been done wilfully and arbitrarily by an angry whim, they were presently released. Also, upon the arrival of the king, John archbishop of Canterbury* was publicly accused of ingratitude

* John Stratford, since 1333 archbishop of Canterbury, and his brother Robert, since 1337 bishop of Chichester, had acted as chancellors alternately for the last ten years.

and other offences by William of Killesby by word of mouth at the Guildhall at London, and afterwards by royal letters; from which charges he declared he was ready to clear himself at the parliament then following, as will appear below. . .

Soon after his arrival the king removed all the sheriffs and other officers and put others in their stead even against their will; and he made a certain knight chancellor of England, namely Robert of Bourchier, and another treasurer, namely first the lord Robert of Sadyton, and afterwards the lord Robert Parvenk, and took the counsel of the young contemning the counsel of the elders. And he ordained that in each county justices should sit, and make enquiry about the collection of the tenth, and of the fifteenth, and of the wool, and all others. And in each county he ordained one great justice, namely an earl or a great baron, to whom he joined others of middle estate; and these justices acted so severely and wilfully that no one escaped unhurt, whether he had done the king's business well or ill: so that without any offence all, even without being indicted or accused, must redeem themselves at excessive fines, if they wished to escape imprisonment, nor would they allow anyone to prove his innocence.

1341.—How the king held his parliament at London and of certain statutes there passed.

Murimuth, p. 112.

(In this parliament the king was obliged to recognise the right of peers to be tried by their peers, as well as to promise that accounts should be audited and ministers sworn to do justice, in parliament. But this statute he revoked the same year.)

In the year of our Lord 1341, in the 15th year of king Edward the third from the Conquest, that king held his parliament at London a fortnight after Easter, wherein the prelates, earls, and great men, to wit the peers and commonalty of the realm, joined in making many good petitions on behalf of the community of the realm, and especially that the Great Charter and the charter of the forest, and the liberties of the church should be wholly maintained; and that those who offended against them, even if they were officers of the king, should be punished, and that the greater officers of the king should be elected by the peers of the realm in parliament. To these the king with his privy council long refused to consent, and so the parliament lasted to the vigil of Whitsunday. But finally the king granted the greater part of the said petitions, but did not grant the appointment and election of his officers; he finally however conceded that the officials should swear in parliament that they would do justice in all their offices, and that if they did not do this, they should resign their offices, on the third day after the beginning of parliament and reply to all their accusers, and that the guilty should be punished by the judgment of their peers. Upon all which and other matters a statute was made and sealed with the king's seal. And then license was given to the prelates and others to leave; but the bishops of Durham and Salisbury, the earls of Salisbury, Warwick, and Northampton were assigned to hear the answer of the archbishop to the charges brought against him and to report to the king in the next parliament. And although the archbishop said he was ready to immediately shew and prove himself innocent, these earls and barons declared they had not then leisure; and so the business remained in suspense.

1341.—Writ revoking a statute.

Rymer, 1177.

The king, to the sheriff of Lincoln, greeting. Whereas in our parliament assembled at Westminster, on the fifteenth day of Easter last past, certain articles expressly contrary to the laws and customs of our realm of England, and to our royal right and prerogatives, are pretended to have been conceded by us by manner of statute:

We, considering how we are bound by oath to observe and defend such laws, customs, rights, and prerogatives, and therefore wishing to recall to the due state those things which have been improvidently done, have taken counsel and have treated upon this with the earls, barons, and otherwise men of our realm:

And because we never consented to the issue of the pretended statute, but having first protested that we would recall the said statute if it actually proceeded, to avoid the perils which it was then feared would arise from refusal since that parliament would otherwise have dissolved in discord without having done anything, and so our arduous business would have been truly ruined, we dissembled as was

GATE OF THE CASTLE OF HENNEBON.

fitting, and permitted the pretended statute to be then sealed; it seemed good to the said earls, barons, and wise men that, since the aforesaid pretended statute did not proceed from our free will, it should be null, and ought not to have the name or force of a statute:

And, therefore, the said statute, with their counsel and consent, we decree to be null and have judged that so far as it has gone it ought to be annulled:

Desiring, however, that the articles contained in the said pretended statute which have been previously approved by other statutes of us or our progenitors, kings of England, shall be observed, according to the form of the said statutes, in all things, as is fitting. And this only we do for the preservation and restoration of the rights of our crown as we are bound, not that we would in any way oppress or grieve our subjects, whom we wish to rule in mildness.

And, therefore, we order you that you cause all this to be publicly proclaimed in such places within your district as you see to be suitable.

Witness the king at Westminster, the first day of October. By the king and council.

Similar writs were directed to all the sheriffs throughout England.

1342.—How the countess of Montfort defended Hennebon.

Froissart, ch. 80 (I. §§ 165-166). *Jehan le Bel*, ch. 54.

(The duchy of Brittany was disputed between John of Montfort, who was supported by Edward of England, and Charles of Blois, supported by Philip of France. Montfort had been taken prisoner, but his wife Joan gallantly carried on the struggle. For the rival claims, see *Appendix*.)

. . . . The countess herself wore harness on her body, and rode on a great charger from street to street, desiring her people to make good defence ; and she caused damsels and other women to cut short their kirtles and to carry stones and pots full of chalk to the walls, to be cast down to their enemies. This lady did there a hardy enterprise. She mounted up to the height of a tower to see how the Frenchmen were ordered without; she saw how that the lords and all the other people of the host were all gone out of their camp to the assault. She issued out with her company and dashed into the French lodgings, and cut down tents and set fire to their lodgings. She found no defence there but certain varlets and boys who ran away. When the lords of France looked behind them and saw their lodgings afire and heard the cry and noise there, they returned to the camp, crying, "Treason! treason!" so that all the assault was left. When the countess saw that, she drew together her company, and when she saw she could not enter again into the town without great damage, she took another way and went to the castle of Brest, the which was not far thence. When sir Louis of Spain, who was marshal of the host, was come to the camp and saw the countess and her company going away he followed after her with a great number; he chased her so near that he slew and hurt divers of them that were behind, evil horsed. But the countess and the most part of her company rode so well that they came to Brest, and there they were received with great joy. . . . . The next day the lords of France, who had lost their tents and their provisions, then took counsel to lodge in bowers of trees nearer to the town, and they had great marvel when they knew that the countess herself had done that enterprise. They of the town wist not where the countess was gone, whereof they were in great trouble, for it was five days ere they heard any tidings. The countess did so much at Brest that she got together five hundred spears; and then about midnight she departed from Brest and by the sun rising she came along by the one side of the host and came to one of the gates of Hennebon, the which was opened for her; and therein she entered and all her company with great noise of trumpets, whereof the French host had great marvel, and armed themselves and ran to the town to assault it, and they within were ready to defend. There began a fierce assault and endured till noon, but the Frenchmen lost more than they within. . . . .

(Some time after, the town was so hard pressed that those within thought of yielding. But just as they are about to give up the town),

Then the countess looked down along the sea out at a window in the castle and began to smile for great joy that she had to see the succours coming, the which she had so long desired. Then she cried out aloud and said twice, "I see the succours of England coming!" Then they of the town ran to the walls and saw a great number of ships, great and small, freshly decked, coming towards Hennebon. They knew well it was the succours of England, who had been on the sea sixty days by reason of contrary winds.

1344.—Of the order of St. George that king Edward established in the castle of Windsor.

Froissart, ch. 100.

In this season the king of England took pleasure to new re-edify the castle of Windsor. . . . . Then king Edward determined to make an order and a brotherhood of a certain number of knights, and to be called knights of the blue garter; and a feast to be kept yearly at Windsor on St. George's day. And to begin this order the king assembled together earls, lords, and knights of his realm and shewed them his intention; and they all joyously agreed to his pleasure, because they saw it was a thing much honourable and whereby great amity and love should grow and increase. Then were there chosen out a certain number of the valiantest men of the realm, and they swore to maintain the ordinances such as were devised; and the king made a chapel in the castle of Windsor, of St. George, and stablished certain canons there to serve God, and endowed them with fair rent. Then the king sent to publish this feast by his heralds, into France, Scotland, Burgundy, Hainault, Flanders, Brabant, and into the empire of Almayne, giving to every knight and squire that would come to the said feast, 15 days of safe conduct before the feast and after the feast, to begin at Windsor on St. George's day next after, in the year of our Lord 1344, and the queen to be there, accompanied with 300 ladies and damsels, all of noble lineage and apparelled accordingly.

1345. — Of the death of Jacques d'Artevelde of Ghent.

Froissart, ch. 115 (1. § 237).

(The truces were ill observed and a renewal of the war was inevitable. Edward therefore crossed to Flanders and attempted to secure a firm basis of operations in Flanders by getting his son accepted as its earl).

In this season reigned in Flanders, in great prosperity and puissance, Jacques d'Artevelde of Ghent, who was as great with the king of England as he could desire: and he had promised the king to make him lord and heritor of Flanders, and to endue his son, the prince of Wales, therewith, and to make the county of Flanders a dukedom. For which cause about the feast of St. John Baptist, 1345, the king of England was come to Sluys, and had brought thither the young prince. The king with all his navy lay in the haven of Sluys, and thither came to visit him his friends of Flanders; then were great councils between the king and Jacques d'Artevelde on the one side, and the councils of the good men of Flanders on the other; so that they of the country were not agreed with the king nor with Jacques d'Artevelde, who preached to them that they should disinherit the earl Louis, their own natural lord and also his young son Louis. And so the last day of their council on the king's great ship the Katherine, they gave a final answer by common accord and said, "Sir, ye have desired us to a thing that is great and weighty, which hereafter may sore touch the county of Flanders and our heirs. Truly we know not at this day no person in the world that we love the preferment of, so much as we do yours. But, sir, this thing we cannot do alone, without that all the commonalty of Flanders accord to the same; sir, we will go home, and every man speak with his company in every town, and as the most part may agree we shall be content; and within a month we shall be here with you again, and then give you a full answer." Jacques d'Artevelde tarried a little season, with the king, and still he promised the king to bring them to his intent; but he was deceived, for as soon as he came to Ghent he went no more out again; for such of Ghent as had been at Sluys at the council there, when they were returned to Ghent, ere Jacques d'Artevelde was come into the town, great and small they assembled in the market place, and then it was openly shewed what request the king of England had made to them, by the setting on of Jacques d'Artevelde; then every man began to murmur against Jacques, for that request pleased them nothing.

When Jacques returned, he came to Ghent about noon. They of the town knew of his coming, and many were assembled in the street where he should pass, and when they saw him they began to murmur and said, "Behold yonder great master, that will order all Flanders after his pleasure, which is not to be suffered." Also then were words sown through all the town, how he had nine years assembled all the revenues of Flanders without any account given, and thereby had kept his state, and also sent great riches out of the country into England secretly. These words set them of Ghent on fire, and as he rode through the street he perceived there was some new matter against him, for such as were wont to make reverence to him he saw them turn their backs towards him and enter into their houses. Then he began to doubt; and as soon as he had alighted at his lodging, he closed fast his gates, doors, and windows. This was scant done before the street was full of men, and specially of them of the small crafts. They assailed his house both behind and before, and the house was broken into. He and his within defended themselves a long space, and slew and hurt many without; but finally he could not endure, for three parts of the men of the town were at the assault. When Jacques saw that he was so sore oppressed, he came to a window, with great humility, bare-headed, and said with fair language, "Good people, what aileth you? why be ye so sore troubled against me? in what manner have I displeased you? shew me and I will make you amends." Then such as heard him answered all with one voice, "We will have account made of the great treasure of Flanders that ye have sent out of the way, without any title of reason." Then Jacques answered meekly, "Certainly, sirs, of the treasure of Flanders I never took anything: withdraw yourselves patiently into your houses and come again to-morrow in the morning, and I shall give you so good account that of reason ye shall be content." Then all they answered and said, "Nay, we will have account given immediately, ye shall not escape us so; we know for truth that ye have sent great riches into England, without our knowledge; wherefore ye shall die." When he heard that word, he joined his hands together, and sore weeping said, "Sirs, such as I am ye have made me, and ye have sworn to me, ere this, to defend me against all persons, and now ye would slay me without reason; ye may do it, an ye will, for I am but one man among you all. For God's sake take better advice, and remember the time past. Ye know right well merchandise was nigh lost in all this country, and by my means it is recovered. I have governed you in great peace and rest, for ye have had all things that ye could wish, corn, riches, and all other merchandise." Then they all cried with one voice, "Come down to us, and preach not so high, and give us account of the great treasure of Flanders." When Jacques saw that he could not appease them, he drew in his head, and closed his window, and so thought to steal out on the back side into a church that joined to his house, but his house was so broken that four hundred persons were entered into his house, and finally then he was taken and slain without mercy, and one Thomas Denys gave him his death stroke.

Thus Jacques d' Artevelde ended his days, who had been a great master in Flanders: poor men first mounteth up, and unhappy men slayeth them at the end.

(Edward thereupon returned to England).

1345. — Of the failure of the great and powerful company of the Bardi.

Giovanni Villani, Istorie Fiorentine, l. xii., c. liv.

In the year 1345 in the month of January failed the company of the Bardi, who had been the greatest merchants in Italy. And the reason was that they, like the Peruzzi, had lent their money and that invested with them to king Edward of England and to the king of Sicily; and that the Bardi found they had owing to them from the king of England, what with capital and interest and gifts promised by him, 900,000 florins of gold,* and on account of his war with the king of France he was unable to pay; and from the king of Sicily 100,000 florins of gold. And to the Peruzzi were owing from the king of England 600,000 florins of gold, and from the king of Sicily 100,000 florins of gold, and a debt of 350,000 florins of gold, so they must stop payment to citizens and foreigners, to whom the Bardi alone owed more than 550,000 florins of gold. Whereby many other smaller companies and individuals whose money was in the hands of the Bardi or Peruzzi or others who had failed, were ruined and so became bankrupt. By this failure of the Bardi, Peruzzi, Acciajuoli, and

* The florin was one-eighth of an ounce of gold.

Bonaccorsi . . of the company of Uzzano Perandoli, and many other small companies and individual craftsmen, owing to the burdens on the state and the disordered loans to lords, of which I have made mention (though not of all, which were too long to tell), came greater ruin and discomfiture to our city of Florence than any our state had received, if the reader well consider the damage caused by such a loss of treasure and money lost by our citizens, and lent from avarice to lords. O cursed and greedy usury, full of the vice of avarice reigning in our blind and mad citizens of Florence, who from covetousness to gain from great lords put their wealth and that of others in their power and lordship to lose, and ruin our republic; for there remained no substance of money in our citizens, except in a few craftsmen and lenders who with their usury consumed and gained for themselves the scattered poverty of our citizens and subjects. But not without cause come to states and citizens the secret judgments of God, to punish the sins which have been committed, as Christ with his own mouth said in the gospel "Ye shall die in your sin." The Bardi agreed to give up to their creditors their possessions, which they estimated would come to 9 shillings and 3 pence in the pound, but at a fair price did not come to six shillings in the pound

1346.—How the king of England came over the sea again.

Froissart, ch. 121. (1. §§ 254-5.)

(In spite of a victory of the earl of Derby at Auberoche, in

1345, the French seemed about to conquer Guienne and were besieging Aiguillon.)

The king of England, who had heard how his men were sore constrained in the castle of Aiguillon, thought to go over the sea into Gascony with a great army. In the same season, the lord Godfrey of Harcourt, who was banished out of France, came into England. He was well received with the king, and retained to be about him, and had fair lands assigned him in England to maintain his degree. Then the king caused a great navy of ships to be ready in the haven of [South] Hampton, and caused all manner of men of war to draw thither. About the feast of St. John Baptist, the year of our Lord God, 1346, the king departed from the queen, and left her in the guiding of the earl of Kent his cousin, and he stablished the lord Percy and the lord Neville to be wardens of his realm, with the archbishop of York, the bishop of Lincoln and the bishop of Durham; for he never left his realm but he left ever enough at home to keep and defend his realm, if need were. Then the king rode to Hampton and there tarried for wind. Then he entered into his ship, and the prince of Wales with him, the lord Godfrey of Harcourt, and all other lords, barons, and knights, with all their companies; they were in number four thousand men of arms, and ten thousand archers, beside Irishmen and Welshmen that followed the host afoot. Thus they sailed forth that day, in the name of God. They were well on their way toward Gascony, but on the third day there arose a contrary wind and drave them on Cornwall, and there they lay at anchor six days. In that space the king had other counsel from sir Godfrey Harcourt. He counselled the king not to go to Gascony, but rather to set a-land in Normandy, and said, " Sir, the country of Normandy is one of the plenteous countries of the world. On jeopardy of my head, if ye will land there, there is none that will resist you; the people of Normandy have not been used to the war, and all the knights and squires of the country are now at the siege before Aiguillon. And sir, there ye shall find great towns that be not walled, whereby your men shall have such winning that they shall be the better thereby twenty years after." The king who was then but in the flower of his youth, desiring nothing so much as to have deed of arms, inclined greatly to the saying of the lord of Harcourt whom he called cousin; then he commanded the mariners to set their course to Normandy and arrived in the isle of Cotentin, at a port called la Hogue.

(He took Caen, and then marched east to join the Flemings; but Philip, who had gathered a great army and in vain tried to prevent his crossing the Seine, came up with him at Crecy, near Abbeville).

1346, Aug.—Of the order of the Englishmen at Crecy.

Froissart, ch. 128 (I. § 274).

On the Friday the king of England lay in the fields, for the country was plentiful in wines and other victual, and if need had been they had provision following in carts and other carriages. That night the king made a supper to all his chief lords of his host, and made them good cheer. And when they were all departed to take their rest, then the king entered into his oratory, and kneeled down before the altar, praying God devoutly that if he fought the next day he might achieve the enterprise to his honour. Then about midnight he laid him down to rest. And in the morning he rose betimes and heard mass, and the prince his son with him, and the most part of his company were confessed and houseled. And, after the mass said, he commanded every man to be armed, and to draw to the field to the same place before appointed. Then the king caused a fenced place to be made by the wood side, behind his host, and there were set all carts and carriages, and within this park were all their horses, for every man was afoot. And into this park there was but one entry. Then he ordained three lines of battle. In the first was the young prince of Wales, and with him was the earl of Warwick and divers other knights and squires. They were eight hundred men of arms and two thousand archers, and a thousand others with the Welshmen; every lord drew to the field appointed under his own banner and pennon. In the second line of battle was the earl of Northampton, the earl of Arundel, and divers others, about eight hundred men of arms and twelve hundred archers. The third line had the king; he had seven hundred men of arms and two thousand archers. Then the king leapt on a palfrey with a white rod in his hand, one of his marshals on the one hand and the other on the other hand; he rode from rank to rank, desiring every man to take heed that day to his right and honour. He spake it so sweetly and with so good countenance and merry cheer that all such as were discomfited took courage in the seeing and hearing of him. And when he had thus visited each line of battle, it was then nine of the day. Then he caused every man to eat and drink a little, and so they did at their leisure. And afterwards they ordered again their battles; then every man lay down on the earth, and by him his helmet and bow, to be the fresher when their enemies should come.

1346.—The order of the Frenchmen at Crecy and how they beheld the demeanour of the Englishmen.

Froissart, ch. 129 (1. §§ 275-7). *Jehan le Bel*, ch. 72.

This Saturday the French king rose betimes and heard mass in Abbeville, in his lodging in the abbey of Saint Peter; and he departed after the sunrising. When he was out of the town two leagues, approaching toward his enemies, some of his lords said to him, "Sir, it were good that you arranged your lines of battle, and let all your foot men pass somewhat on before, that they be not troubled with the horsemen." Then the king sent four knights, ... to ride to view the English host. And so they rode so near that they might well see part of their dealing. The Englishmen saw them well, and knew well how they were come thither to view them; they let them alone, and made no countenance

toward them, and let them return as they came.
And when the French king saw these four knights
return again, he tarried till they came to him, and
said, "Sirs, what tidings?" These four knights each
of them looked on the other, for there was none
would speak before his companion; finally, the king
said to Moine, who belonged to the king of Bohemia,
and had done in his days so much that he was
reputed for one of the valiantest knights of the
world, "Sir, speak you." Then he said, "Sir, I shall
speak since it pleaseth you, under the correction of
my fellows. Sir, we have ridden and seen the behaving
of your enemies; know you that they are rested
in three lines of battle, abiding for you. Sir, I will
counsel you, as for my part, saving your displeasure,
that you and all your company rest here and lodge
for this night; for ere they that be behind of your
company be come hither, and ere your lines be set
in good order it will be very late, and your people
be weary and out of array, and you shall find your
enemies fresh and ready to receive you. Early in
the morning you may order your lines at more
leisure, and consider your enemies with more
deliberation, and regard well what way ye will
assail them; for, sir, surely they will abide you."
Then the king commanded that it should be done.
Then his two marshals one rode before and another
behind, saying to every banner, "Tarry and abide
here in the name of God and Saint Denis." They
that were foremost tarried, but they that were
behind would not tarry but rode forth, and said

how they would in no wise abide until they were as far forward as the foremost. And when they before saw them come on behind, then they rode forward again, so that neither the king nor his marshals could rule them; so they rode without order or good array till they came in sight of their enemies. . . . . When they saw that they were near to their enemies, they took their swords and cried, "Down with them! let us slay them all!" There was no man, though he were present at the journey, that could imagine or show the truth of the evil order that was among the French party, and yet they were a marvellous great number. What I write in this book, I learned it specially of the Englishmen who well beheld their dealing, and also certain knights of sir John of Hainault, who was always about king Philip, shewed me as they knew.

1346.—Of the battle of Crecy between the king of England and the French king.

Froissart, ch. 130 (I. §§ 277-280, 283).

The Englishmen, who were in three lines of battle lying on the ground to rest them, as soon as they saw the Frenchmen approach, rose upon their feet, fair and easily without any haste, and arranged their lines. The first was the prince's division; the archers there stood in manner of a harrow, and the men of arms in the bottom of the division. The earl of Northampton and the earl of Arundel with the second line were on a wing in good order, ready to comfort the prince's line if need were. The lords

BATTLE OF CRECY

and knights of France came not to the assembly together in good order, for some came before and some came after, in such haste and evil order that one of them did trouble another. When the French king saw the Englishmen, his blood changed, and he said to his marshals, "Make the Genoese go on before and begin the battle, in the name of God and Saint Denis." There were of the Genoese crossbowmen about fifteen thousand; but they were so weary of going afoot that day six leagues armed with their crossbows, that they said to their constables, "We be not well ordered to fight this day, for we be not in the case to do any great deed of arms; we have more need of rest." These words came to the earl of Alençon, who said, "A man is well at ease to be charged with such a sort of rascals, who faint and fail now at most need." Also the same season there fell a great rain, with thunder and lightning very great and horrible. And before the rain there came flying over both armies a great number of crows for fear of the tempest coming. Then anon the air began to wax clear, and the sun to shine fair and bright; the which was right in the Frenchmen's eyes, and on the Englishmen's backs. When the Genoese were assembled together and began to approach, they made a great leap and cry to abash the Englishmen, but they stood still and stirred not for all that. Then the Genoese again, the second time, made another leap and a fell cry, and stepped forward a little, and the Englishmen removed not one foot. Thirdly again they leapt and cried and went forth till they came within shot. Then they shot fiercely with their crossbows. Then the English archers stept forth one pace and let fly their arrows altogether, and so thick that it seemed snow. When the Genoese felt the arrows piercing through heads, arms, and breasts, many of them cast down their crossbows, and did cut their strings, and returned discomfited. When the French king saw them flee away, he said, "Slay these rascals, for they will hinder and trouble us without reason." Then you should have seen the men of arms dash in among them, and they killed a great number of them. And ever still the Englishmen shot as they saw thickest press; the sharp arrows ran into the men of arms and into their horses; and many fell, horse and men, among the Genoese; and when they were down they could not rise again; the press was so thick that one overthrew another. And also among the Englishmen there were certain rascals that went afoot, with great knives, and they went in among the men of arms, and slew and murdered many as they lay on the ground, both earls, barons, knights, and squires; whereof the king of England was after displeased, for he had rather they had been taken prisoners. The valiant king of Bohemia, called John of Luxemburg, son to the noble emperor Henry of Luxemburg, for all that he was nigh blind, when he understood the order of the battle, he said to them about him, "Where is the lord Charles my son?" His men said, "Sir, we cannot tell; we think he is fighting." Then he said, "Sirs, ye are my men,

WINDMILL HILL AT CRECY.

my companions and friends in this enterprise; I
require you bring me so forward that I may strike
one stroke with my sword." They said they would
do his commandment; and to the intent that they
should not lose him in the press, they tied all their
reins of their bridles each to other, and set the king
before to accomplish his desire; and so they went
on their enemies. The lord Charles, his son, who
wrote himself king of Germany, came in good order
to the battle; but when he saw the matter went awry
on their part, he departed I cannot tell you which
way. The king his father was so far forward that he
struck a stroke with his sword, yea and more than
four, and fought valiantly. And so did his company,
and they adventured themselves so forward that they
were all slain, and the next day they were found in
the place about the king, and all their horses tied
each to other. . . . .
The day of the battle certain Frenchmen and
Germans perforce opened the archers of the prince's
battalion, and came and fought with the men at
arms, hand to hand. Then the second division of
the Englishmen came to succour the prince's
division, the which was time, for they had then
much ado. And they with the prince sent a
messenger to the king, who was on a little windmill
hill. Then the knight said to the king, "Sir, the
earl of Warwick, sir Reynold Cobham, and other
such as be about the prince, your son, are fiercely
fought withal and are sore handled; wherefore they
desire you that you and your division will come

and aid them, for if the Frenchmen increase, as they fear they will, your son and they shall have much ado." Then the king said, " Is my son dead, or hurt, or on the earth felled?" "No, sir," quoth the knight, " but he is hardly matched, wherefore he hath need of your aid." "Well," said the king, "return to him and to them that sent you hither, and say to them that they send no more to me for any adventure that falleth, so long as my son is alive; and also say to them that they suffer him this day to win his spurs, for, if God be pleased, I will this day to be his and the honour thereof, and to them that be about him." Then the knight returned again to them and shewed the king's words, the which greatly encouraged them; and they repined in that they had sent to the king as they did. . . . .
In the evening the French king had left about him no more than threescore persons, whereof sir John of Hainault was one, who had remounted once the king, for his horse was slain with an arrow. Then sir John of Hainault said to the king, " Sir, depart hence, for it is time; lose not yourself wilfully. If you have lost at this time, ye shall recover it again another season." And so he took the king's horse by the bridle and led him away in a manner perforce. Then the king rode till he came to the castle of Broyes. The gate was closed, because it was by that time dark. Then the king called the captain, who came to the walls and said, "Who is it that calleth there, this time of night?" Then the king said,

"Open your gate quickly, for this is the fortune of France." The captain knew then it was the king, and opened the gate and let down the bridge. The king would not tarry there, but drank and departed thence about midnight; and so rode by such guides as knew the country well till he came in the morning to Amiens, and there he rested. This Saturday the Englishmen never departed from their ranks for chasing of any man, but kept still their field and ever defended themselves against all such as came to assail them. This battle ended about evensong time.

1346, Oct.—Battle of Neville's Cross.

Chron. of Lanercost, 347-357.

(After the English had failed to take Dunbar, the party of Bruce in Scotland had re-won the greater part of the kingdom, and in 1341 the young David Bruce returned from France. Edward again led an army into Scotland, but could effect nothing; and in March, 1345, a truce was agreed to. In the summer of 1346 at the instigation of Philip of France, David invaded the Northern counties of England, but was met near Durham by the archbishop of York and lords Neville and Percy, the wardens of the Border).

Now on the fourteenth day of October the bishop set out with his host from Richmond, and marched with all speed by the straight way unto Castle Barnard; on the morrow, in the neighbourhood of this same castle, he and the other chiefs held a reckoning of their men of arms, horsemen and footmen, knights and esquires; for there was there a little hill having a level summit. Moreover in the same place the commanders did ordain the arraying of the host, and all else that was fitting. Accordingly they parted themselves into three strong divisions, whereof the lord Henry Percy led the first, the lord Thomas of Rokeby the second, but the third the bishop of York himself commanded, like a wise father, a pure and holy shepherd of his sheep. And so all the host, not in hatred as was Cain when he slew his brother, nor yet in vain glory as was Absalom when the tree caught him up, marched with due care towards the town of Auckland, putting their trust not in sword or helm, in spear or hauberk, or other golden armour, but altogether upon the name of Christ, and knowing beside that they were not going to attack others, but to resist them that had come against them: and that same night they pitched their tents in a certain fair wood and there the army of England awaited the day. Now at the dawning of the morrow, which was the vigil of St. Luke the evangelist, William of Douglas and fifty others with him went forth from the Scottish host to harry the country and get them plunder; whereby it came to pass that the spoil, which the Scotch took in the morning, the English parted among themselves in the evening. For on that morning, while the Scots were wasting the village of Merrington, there fell on them suddenly tempestuous weather and dense clouds. Besides this, there came to their ears the tramp of steeds and the clash of armour, whence there fell on them so sudden a plague of fear that William and all his men knew not whither they should turn. So, as God willed, smitten with terror at this sudden chance, they stumbled upon the division of the lord archbishop of York and the lord Thomas of Rokeby. Thereby many of them were slain, but William and two hundred with him, who were on tried horses, escaped for that time, though not unhurt. Then Robert of Ogle, a man of great strength, and by no means untrained in the arts of war, followed after them over hill and plain, and many he slew with his own hand, nor would he stay until his steed, out-worn by exceeding toil, stopped at a great stream at the bottom of a wooded vale and could go no further. Then came William much heated to the Scottish host, and cried aloud with much fervor of heart: "David, quick up! all the Englishmen are upon us." But David made answer that it could not be; "There are not left," he said, "in England but wretched monks, impious priests, swineherds, tailors, and cobblers; these dare not face me, I am safe enough"; nathless they faced him, and, as was afterwards made plain, handled him right well. "Of a truth," answered William, "most honoured king, saving your peace, you will not find it so; they are many and mighty men, and come against us with all speed and are eager after battle." Now, immediately before these words, had come two Black Monks of them of Durham to treat with David for a truce. "See then," said David, "with what guile do these false monks speak with us; therefore did they hold us in conclave, that suddenly the English host should come upon us, thus caught in their toils." Wherefore he bade seize them at once, and behead them, but at that time the Scots were so busied that the monks fled unseen, and with much joy and no harm made their way safely back to their own place. On this wise did David, more foolish than a fool, endeavour to catch the fish, ere he had a net, whereby he lost many and caught but few; nor did he keep to the purpose which he had purposed, and like another Haman or Achitophel, what he had designed for us fell on his own head. Then, viewing his people David gathered the Scots together, (folk that were to be scattered, as the event willed,) and, like a second Jabin against Joshua, arrayed three great and strong divisions to front the Englishmen. In the first rank he set the earl Patrick, but he, like a man of no skill, begged not to have the leadership. And that post the earl of Moray forthwith obtained, and thus in the first rank of the army he held the chief place, and there afterwards he fell in the fray. With him were many valiant men of Scotland, as the earl of Strathern, the earl of Fife, John of Douglas the brother of lord William of Douglas, the lord Alexander of Ramsay, and many other valiant earls and barons, knights and squires, furiously raging, of unbridled spirit, all of one mind against the English, nor would they stay from their headlong course, but firmly trusting in their own power, and rising with overweening pride thought, like Satan, to reach the stars. The second division David the king led himself, not him of whom

the choirs sang that he had turned to flight his ten thousands in the war. With him he brought the earl of Buchan, Malcolm Fleming, lord Alexander of Strathern, the earl of Monteith, and many another, whom we know not, and, did we know, it were tedious to relate. . . . .
About the third hour hard by Durham the English host came upon the Scotchmen, and then in the first line the earl of Angus, a man of noble stock, of great valour and wonderful virtue, was ever ready to do battle for his country, whose fair feats, indeed, not one or many tongues could chronicle. The lord Henry Percy, a good warrior like a second Judas Maccabeus, a man of low stature but great wisdom, boldly set his own body in the foremost ranks and made all bold to spring into the fray. The lord Ralph of Neville, a truth-speaker and a valiant man, bold, wise, and fear-worthy, so fought in that fray that thereafter the dints of his blows were to be seen on the foe. . . . .

In the second division the lord archbishop of York was their leader, who called his sons and gave them his blessing. . . . .

There was also a bishop of the order of the Minorites, who for a blessing bade the Englishmen fight like men on pain of much penance, and ordered that none should spare a Scot. And when he himself met the foe, he spared not for inflicting of penance or for rebuke, but with a certain staff gave them indulgences, penances, and proper absolution; such power had he then that with his staff, without any confession heard, he absolved the Scots of all future trouble in this world. . . . . In the third division was the lord John of Mowbray. . . . . The lord Thomas of Rokeby, like a good leader, pledged the Scots in such liquor as, when they had once tasted, they desired no more trial of it, and stood forth in all men's eyes as an example of one who warred bravely for his country. . . . Thus amid the blare of trumpets, the clashing of shields, the hurtling of arrows, you might have heard spears flying, and the wailing of the wounded. Arms were shattered, heads broken, many, alas, slain on the field. Before the hour of vespers the battle came to an end. The Scots fled and our men slew them; all praise to the Highest, Who on that day gave the victory to the English. And thus, by the prayers of the Blessed Virgin Mary and of Saint Cuthbert, the confessor of Christ, David and the flower of Scotland fell by the just judgment of God into the pit which they themselves had digged. David, who called himself king of Scotland, was taken, and not long after, with many nobler captives, was brought to London and there thrown into prison.

1346 —Song of Neville's Cross.

By Laurence Minot [Political Poems (Rolls Series) 1. 83].

Sir David had of his men great loss
With sir Edward at Neville's Cross.

Sir David the Bruce,
    Would strive, did he say,
To ride through all England,
    For naught would he stay.

At Westminster Hall
    Should his steeds stand
Whilst our king Edward
    Was out of the land.

But now hath sir David
    Missed of his marks,
And Philip of Valois
    With all their great clerks.

Sir Philip the Valois,
    Sooth for to say,
Sent unto sir David
    And fair 'gan him pray,

To ride through all England
    Their foemen to slay,
And said "none is at home
    To hinder the way."

None hinders his way
    To wend where he will,
But with shepherds' staves
    Found he his fill.

From Philip the Valois
    Was sir David sent,
All England to win,
    From Tweed unto Trent.

He brought many bagmen,
    Ready bent was their bow,
They robbed and they ravaged
    And nought they let go.

. . . .

But shamed were the knaves
    And sad must they feel,
For at Neville's Cross
    Needs must they kneel.

Of the archbishop of York
    Now will I begin,
For he may with his right hand
    Absolve us of sin.

Both Durham and Carlisle
    They would never blin*
The worship of England
    With weapons to win.

Mickle worship they won,
    And well have they waken,
For sir David the Bruce
    Was in that time taken.

When sir David the Bruce
    Sat on his steed,
He said of all England
    Had he no dread.

But brave John of Copland,
    A man gay in weed,
Talked to sir David
    And learned him his creed.

        * Cease.

There was sir David,
  So doughty in deed,
The fair town of London
  Had he as his meed.

Soon was sir David
  Brought into the Tower,
And William the Douglas,
  With men of honour.

. . . .

Sir David the Bruce
  Maketh his moan,
The fair crown of Scotland
  All hath he foregone.

He looked unto France
  And help had he none
Of sir Philip the Valois
  Nor yet of sir John.

. . . .

The Scots with their falsehood
  Thus went they about
All for to win England
  Whilst Edward was out.

1346. — How Douglas breakfasted at Tynemouth.

Chronicle of St. Albans, ii. 378.

Now heavier troubles came on Thomas, the prior of Tynemouth; for the king of Scotland, called David the Bruce, taking courage at the absence of king Edward, who at that time was fighting against Philip king of France at Crecy, and prompted by letters from the said Philip, collected an army, entered the country, killed several, captured many, burnt farms, destroyed provisions, demanded ransom for goods, and did innumerable evils. But Thomas, amid these dangers, remained unbent, and put his priory in readiness with men, arms, provisions, and instruments of war, in such a way that the enemy would not be able to do hurt without great difficulty and peril to themselves.

At that time William Douglas, the leader of the army, on which was placed all the hope of the Scots, being a haughty, arrogant, and sarcastic man, sent a message to Thomas after his fashion, telling him to get breakfast ready, for in two days he was going to breakfast with him, so saying of a truth but to frighten him. And his saying was fulfilled—for it was a prophecy like that saying of Caiaphas. For two days after, he was taken prisoner, and sent to Tynemouth for safe custody. The prior went to meet him, and jestingly bade him welcome to the breakfast he had prepared. Whereat William, "I'm very angry at coming in this way." "Nay," said the prior," you could never be more welcome."

1347, Aug.—How the town of Calais was given up to the king of England.

Froissart, ch. 146 (I. § 311). *Jehan le Bel*, chs. 90-91.

(Immediately after Crecy, Edward had laid siege to Calais. Philip came with an army in the spring of the next year, but was unable to deliver the town, and withdrew.)

After that the French king was thus departed from

Sangate, they within Calais saw well how their succour failed them, for the which they were in great sorrow. Then they desired so much their captain, sir John of Vienne, that he went to the walls of the town, and made a sign to speak with some person of the host. When the king heard thereof he sent thither sir Walter of Manny and sir Basset. Then sir John of Vienne said to them, "Sirs, ye be right valiant knights in deeds of arms, and ye know well how the king, my master, hath sent me and others to this town and commanded us to keep it on his behalf, in such wise that we take no blame nor do him no damage; and we have done all that lieth in our power. Now our succours have failed us, and we are sore straitened that we have not wherewithal to live, but we must all die or else go mad with famine, without the noble and gentle king of yours will take mercy on us. Wherefore, we beseech you to desire him to have pity on us, and to let us go and depart as we are, and let him take the town and castle and all the goods that are therein, of which there is great abundance."

Then sir Walter of Manny said, "Sir, we know somewhat of the intention of the king, our master, for he hath shewed it unto us. Surely know for truth it is not his mind that ye nor they within the town should depart so, for it is his will that ye should put yourselves into his pure will to ransom all such as pleaseth him, and to put to death such as he list; for they of Calais have done him such contraries and despites, and have caused him to spend so much of his goods, and has lost so many of his men, that he is sore grieved against them."

Then the captain said, "Sir, this is too hard a matter to us. We are here within but a small number of knights and squires, who have truly served the king, our master, as well as you serve yours in like case. And we have endured much pain and unease; but we will yet endure as much pain as ever knight did, rather than to consent that the worst lad in the town should have any more evil than the greatest of us all. Therefore, sir, we pray you of your humility yet that you will go and speak to the king of England, and desire him to have pity on us; for we trust to find in him so much gentleness, that by the grace of God his purpose shall change." Sir Walter of Manny and sir Basset returned to the king and declared to him all that had been said. The king said he would none otherwise, but that they should yield them up simply to his pleasure. Then sir Walter said, "Sir, saving your displeasure in this, you may be in the wrong, for you shall give by this an evil example. If you send any of us your servants into any fortress, we will not be very glad to go, if you put any of them in the town to death after they have yielded, for in likewise they will deal with us if the case chanced alike." The which words divers other lords that were present sustained and maintained. Then the king said, "Sirs, I will not be alone against you all; therefore, sir Walter of Manny, you shall go and say to the captain that all the grace that he shall find now in me is, that they let six of the chief burgesses of the town come out bare-headed, bare-footed, and bare-legged and in their shirts, with halters about their necks, with the keys of the town and castle in their hands; and let these six yield themselves purely to my will, and the residue I will take to mercy." Then sir Walter returned and found sir John of Vienne still on the wall, abiding for an answer. Then sir Walter shewed him all the grace that he could get of the king. "Well," quoth sir John, "Sir, I beseech you tarry here a certain space till I go into the town and shew this to the commons of the town, who sent me hither." Then sir John went into the Market Place and sounded the common bell. Then forthwith men and women assembled there; then the captain made report of all that he had done, and said, "Sirs, it will be none otherwise, therefore now take advice and make a short answer." Then all the people began to weep and to make such sorrow, that there was not so hard a heart if they had seen them, but that would have had great pity of them; the captain himself wept piteously. At last the most rich burgess of all the town, called Eustace of Saint Peter's, rose up and said openly, "Sirs, great and small, great mischief it should be to suffer to die such people as are in this town, either by famine or otherwise, when there is a way to save them. I think he or they should have great merit of our Lord God that might keep them from such mischief. As for my part I have good trust in our Lord God that if I die to save the residue, that God will pardon me. Wherefore, to save them, I will be the first to put my life in jeopardy." When he had thus said, every man worshipped him and divers kneeled down at his feet with sore weeping and sore sighs. Then another honest burgess rose and said, "I will keep company with my gossip Eustace." He was called John Daire. Then rose up Jacques of Wisant, who was rich in goods and heritage; he said also he would hold company with his two cousins; likewise so did Peter Wisant, his brother. And then rose two others and said they would do the same. Then they went and apparelled them as the king desired.

Then the captain went with them to the gate; there was great lamentation made of men, women, and children at their departing. Then the gate was opened and he issued out with the six burgesses and closed the gate again, for that they were between the gate and the barriers. Then he said to sir Walter of Manny, "Sir, I deliver here to you as captain of Calais, by the whole consent of all the people of the town, these six burgesses. And I swear to you truly that they are to-day the most honourable, rich, and most notable burgesses of all the town of Calais. Wherefore, gentle knight, I beseech you pray the king have mercy on them that they die not." Quoth sir Walter, "I can not say what the king will do, but I shall do for them the best I can." Then the barriers were opened; the six burgesses went

CALAIS.

towards the king, and the captain entered again into the town. When sir Walter presented these burgesses to the king they kneeled down and held up their hands and said, "Gentle king, behold here we six, who were burgesses in Calais and great merchants, have brought to you the keys of the town and of the castle, and we submit ourselves clearly into your will and pleasure to save the residue of the people of Calais, who have suffered great pain. Sir, we beseech your grace to have mercy and pity on us through your high nobleness." Then all the earls and barons and others that were there wept for pity. Then the king looked felly on them, for greatly he hated the people of Calais for the great damages and displeasures they had done him on the sea before. Then he commanded their heads to be stricken off. Then every man besought the king for mercy, but he would hear no man in that behalf. Then sir Walter of Manny said, "Ah! noble king, for God's sake refrain your wrath; you have the name of sovereign nobleness, therefore now do not a thing that should blemish your renown, nor give cause to some to speak of you any villany. Every man will say it is a great cruelty to put to death such honest persons, who by their own wills put themselves into your grace to save their company." Then the king turned away from him, and commanded to send for the hangmen, and said, "They of Calais have caused many of my men to be slain, wherefore these shall die in like wise." Then the queen, being great with child, kneeled down and sore weeping said, "Ah!

gentle sir, since I passed the sea in great peril I have desired nothing of you, therefore I now humbly pray you in honour of the Son of the Virgin Mary, and for the love of me, that you will take mercy of these six burgesses." The king beheld the queen, and stood still in thought a space, and then said, "Ah! dame, I would you had been now in some other place; you make such request of me that I cannot deny you. Wherefore I give them to you to do your pleasure with them." Then the queen caused them to be brought into her chamber, and made the halters to be taken from their necks, and caused them to be new-clothed, and gave them their dinner at their leisure. And then she gave each of them six nobles, and made them to be brought out of the host in safeguard and set at their liberty.

(In Sept. a truce was signed with Philip, and this was repeatedly renewed until 1355.)

1349.—Of the Black Death.

Knighton, 2599.

Then the grievous plague penetrated the seacoasts from Southampton, and came to Bristol, and there almost the whole strength of the town died, struck as it were by sudden death; for there were few who kept their beds more than three days, or two days, or half a day; and after this the fell death broke forth on every side with the course of the sun. There died at Leicester in the small parish of S. Leonard more than 380, in the parish of Holy Cross more than 400; in the parish of S. Margaret of Leicester more than 700; and so in each parish a great number. Then the bishop of Lincoln sent through the whole bishopric, and gave general power to all and every priest, both regular and secular, to hear confessions, and absolve with full and entire episcopal authority except in matters of debt, in which case the dying man, if he could, should pay the debt while he lived, or others should certainly fulfil that duty from his property after his death. Likewise, the pope granted full remission of all sins to whoever was absolved in peril of death, and granted that this power should last till next Easter, and everyone could choose a confessor at his will. In the same year there was a great plague of sheep everywhere in the realm, so that in one place there died in one pasturage more than 5,000 sheep, and so rotted that neither beast nor bird would touch them. And there were small prices for everything on account of the fear of death. For there were very few who cared about riches or anything else. For a man could have a horse, which before was worth 40s., for 6s. 8d., a fat ox for 4s., a cow for 12d., a heifer for 6d., a fat wether for 4d., a sheep for 3d., a lamb for 2d., a big pig for 5d., a stone of wool for 9d. Sheep and cattle went wandering over fields and through crops, and there was no one to go and drive or gather them, so that the number cannot be reckoned which perished in the ditches in every district, for lack of herdsmen; for there was such a lack of servants that no one knew what he ought to do.

In the following autumn no one could get a reaper for less than 8d. with his food, a mower for less than 12d. with his food. Wherefore many crops perished in the fields for want of some one to gather them; but in the pestilence year, as is above said of other things, there was such abundance of all kinds of corn that no one much troubled about it. The Scots, hearing of the cruel pestilence of the English, believed it had come to them from the avenging hand of God, and—as it was commonly reported in England—took for their oath when they wanted to swear, "By the foul death of England." But when the Scots, believing the English were under the shadow of the dread vengeance of God, came together in the forest of Selkirk, with purpose to invade the whole realm of England, the fell mortality came upon them, and the sudden and awful cruelty of death winnowed them, so that about 5,000 died in a short time. Then the rest, some feeble, some strong, determined to return home, but the English followed and overtook them and killed many of them.

Master Thomas of Bradwardine was consecrated by the pope archbishop of Canterbury, and when he returned to England he came to London, but within two days was dead. He was famous beyond all other clerks in the whole of Christendom, especially in theology, but likewise in the other liberal sciences. At the same time priests were in such poverty everywhere that many churches were widowed and lacking the divine offices, masses, mattins, vespers, sacraments, and other rites. A man could scarcely get a chaplain under £10 or 10 marks to minister to a church. And when a man could get a chaplain for 5 or 4 marks or even for two marks with his food when there was an abundance of priests before the pestilence, there was scarcely anyone now who was willing to accept a vicarage for £20 or 20 marks; but within a short time a very great multitude of those whose wives had died in the pestilence flocked into orders, of whom many were illiterate and little more than laymen, except so far as they knew how to read although they could not understand.

Meanwhile the king sent proclamation into all the counties that reapers and other labourers should not take more then they had been accustomed to take, under the penalty appointed by statute. But the labourers were so lifted up and obstinate that they would not listen to the king's command, but if anyone wished to have them he had to give them what they wanted, and either lose his fruit and crops, or satisfy the lofty and covetous wishes of the workmen. And when it was known to the king that they had not observed his command, and had given greater wages to the labourers, he levied heavy fines upon abbots, priors, knights, greater and lesser, and other great folk and small folk of the realm, of some 100s., of some 40s., of some 20s., from each according to what he could give. He took from each carucate* of the realm 20s., and, notwithstanding this, a fifteenth. And afterwards the king had many labourers arrested,

* A hundred acres.

and sent them to prison ; many withdrew themselves and went into the forests and woods ; and those who were taken were heavily fined. Their ringleaders were made to swear that they would not take daily wages beyond the ancient custom, and then were freed from prison. And in like manner was done with the other craftsmen in the boroughs and villages. . . After the aforesaid pestilence, many buildings, great and small, fell into ruins in every city, borough, and village for lack of inhabitants, likewise many villages and hamlets became desolate, not a house being left in them, all having died who dwelt there ; and it was probable that many such villages would never be inhabited. In the winter following there was such a want of servants in work of all kinds, that one would scarcely believe that in times past there had been such a lack. . . . . . And so all necessaries became so much dearer that what in times past had been worth a penny, was then worth 4d. or 5d.

Magnates and lesser lords of the realm who had tenants made abatements of the rent in order that the tenants should not go away on account of the want of servants and the general dearness, some half the rent, some more, some less, some for two years, some for three, some for one year, according as they could agree with them. Likewise, those who received of their tenants daywork throughout the year, as is the practice with villeins, had to give them more leisure, and remit such works, and either entirely to free them, or give them an easier tenure at a small rent, so that homes should not be everywhere irrecoverably ruined, and the land everywhere remain entirely uncultivated.

1349.—Of the death of abbot Michael of St. Alban's.

Chronicle of S. Albans, ii. 369.

(This example of the mortality caused by the Black Death is here given because it throws light on the condition of the most celebrated of English monasteries.)

He had brought much good to the monastery by his labour, when the pestilence came which destroyed almost the half of all flesh, and prevented him with untimely death; his life was cut off, as by a weaver's shears, when it seemed but beginning. He was touched by this common malady among the first of the monks struck by the fatal plague; and although on Sunday he began to feel the sickness of his body, yet moved by the solemnity of the festival and the memory of our Lord's humility, even before breakfast he solemnly celebrated a greater mass, and after mass with due humility and reverence washed the feet of his poor, and after the meal washed and kissed the feet of all the friars, and fulfilled all the duty of that day by himself without any help.

On the morrow, his sickness increasing, he betook himself to his bed, and like a true Catholic, having made a pure confession with contrition of heart, he received the last sacraments of unction; and so with grief and mourning drew out the time till the ninth day of Easter. On which day, while the convent was breakfasting, the hearts of all his monks were saddened by his departure. He had been carried from the false shadows of this world to the true light, from incessant labour to rest, from mourning to the ineffable joy of his Lord. Assuredly during the whole of his life, he was most pious, most compassionate, and, like as we are told of Moses, most mild.

There died at that time, besides those many who were lost at the cells (dependent priories), 47 monks of remarkable piety and learning, most of whom certainly had not their equals in virtue. This we believe was done for this purpose, that a man of angelic name and actions should not appear alone and without companions in the presence of the Judge, a man who his whole life had not ceased to multiply his Lord's talent, and had cleansed so much grain worthy to be carried into the Lord's granary.

But because there is no man on earth who does not sin, nor a son of man who does not offend, so, that he may not be believed entirely free from fault, to his negligence is it to be ascribed, that he pulled down and sold the beautiful hall made by the expense and care of his predecessor at his manor at Tydenhanger, to the no small inconvenience of his successors, and to the notable injury of the place. For this is the nature of almost all prelates who follow others, that they care little for the works of their predecessors, and either destroy their rich buildings or cease to visit them, caring more for other places that their fancy chooses. Yet the holy man must be forgiven, for although indeed he did commit this fault, yet he prepared and carried out innumerable benefits in comparison wherewith the error I have mentioned disappears, like a tiny drop of water thrown amid great flames.

1349.—Of the Flagellants.

Robert of Avesbury, p. 179.

In the year of our Lord 1349, about the feast of S. Michael, more than * men, having for the most part their origin in Zealand and Holland, came from Flanders to London, and sometimes in the church of S. Paul, sometimes in other places of the same city, twice a-day in the sight of the people, clad from thigh to ankle in linen cloth, the rest of the body bare, each having upon his head a cap marked with a red cross before and behind, each holding in the right hand a scourge with three cords, each (cord) having one knot, through the middle of some of which knots sharp nails were fixed, walked one after the other in procession with bare feet, and scourged themselves with these scourges on their bare and bleeding bodies, four of them singing in their language and four replying, like Litanies sung by Christians. In this procession they all thrice prostrated themselves to the ground, with their hands stretched in the shape of a cross, ever singing; and then finally some lay down and others stepped upon them and scourged them with their scourges, and this they did one after the other until the rite had been observed with all of them. Afterwards each put on his usual clothes,

* The number is wanting.

and bearing the caps on their heads and scourges in their hands, they returned to their inns; and did like penance as was said, every night.

1349.—How sir Amery of Pavia, a Lombard, sold the town of Calais, whereof he was captain, to the lord Geoffrey Charny of France.

Froissart, ch. 150 (I. § 317).

All this season in the town of St. Omer was the lord Geoffrey of Charny, who kept the frontiers there. He bethought him how the Lombards naturally be covetous; wherefore he thought to assay to get the town of Calais, whereof Amery of Pavia, a Lombard, was captain. By reason of the truce they of St. Omer might go to Calais, and they of Calais to St. Omer, so that daily they resorted together to do their merchandises. Then sir Geoffrey secretly fell into treaty with sir Amery of Pavia, so that he promised to deliver into the Frenchmen's hands the town and castle of Calais for twenty thousand crowns. This was not done so secretly but that the king of England had knowledge thereof; then the king sent for Amery of Pavia to come into England to Westminster to speak with him, and so he came over, for he thought that the king had not had knowledge of the matter; he thought he had done it so secretly. When the king saw him he took him apart and said, "Thou knowest well I have given thee in keeping the thing in this world that I love best, next my wife and children; that is to say, the town and castle of Calais, and thou hast sold it to the Frenchmen, wherefore thou hast well deserved to die." Then the Lombard knelt down and said, "Ah, noble king, I cry your mercy. It is true that ye say. But, sir, the bargain may well be broken, for as yet I have received never a penny." The king had loved well the Lombard, and said, "Amery, I wish that thou go forward on thy bargain, and let me have knowledge beforehand of the day thou appointest to deliver up the town; and upon this condition I forgive thee thy trespass." . . Then sir Geoffrey of Charny thought well to have Calais, and assembled a certain number secretly, some five hundred spears. There were but a few that knew what he purposed; I think he never made the French king of knowledge thereof; for if he had, I trow the king would not have consented thereto, because of the truce. This Lombard had appointed to deliver the castle the first night of the new year, and sent word thereof by a brother of his to the king of England.

1350.—Of the battle at Calais between the king of England, under the banner of sir Walter of Manny, and sir Geoffrey of Charny and the Frenchmen.

Froissart, ch. 151 (I. §§ 318-9).

When the king of England knew the certain day appointed, he departed out of England with three hundred men of arms and six hundred archers, and took shipping at Dover, and in the evening arrived at Calais, so secretly that no man knew thereof, and laid his men in bushments in the chambers and towers within the castle. Then the king said to sir Walter Manny, "I wish that ye be chief of this enterprise, for I and my son the prince will fight under your banner." The lord Geoffrey of Charny, the last day of December at night, departed from Arras and all his company, and came near to Calais about the hour of midnight, and sent two squires to the postern gate of the castle of Calais, and there they found sir Amery ready. Then they demanded of him if it were time that the lord Geoffrey should come; and the Lombard said, "Yes." Then sir Geoffrey sent twelve knights with a hundred men of arms to go and take possession of the castle of Calais, for he thought well that if he might have the castle he should soon get the town, seeing he had so great a number of men with him and daily might have more. And he delivered to the lord Odoart of Renty twenty thousand crowns to pay the Lombard; and sir Geoffrey remained still in the fields firmly, with his banner before him. The Lombard let down the bridge of the postern and suffered the hundred men to enter peaceably, and sir Odoart delivered at the postern twenty thousand crowns in a bag to the Lombard, who said, "I trust here be all, for I have no leisure now to count them, for it will be day anon." Then he cast the bag with crowns into a coffer, and said to the Frenchmen, "Come on, sirs; ye shall enter into the donjon; then shall you be sure to be lords of the castle." They went thither, and he drew apart the bar, and the gate opened. Within this tower was the king of England with two hundred spears, who issued out with their swords and axes in their hands, crying, "Manny! Manny! to the rescue! What weeneth the Frenchmen with so few men to win the castle of Calais." Then the Frenchmen saw well that defence could not avail them, and yielded themselves prisoners, and they were put into the same tower in prison. And the Englishmen issued out of the castle into the town, and mounted on their horses, for they had all the French prisoners' horses, and rode to the Boulogne gate. There was sir Geoffrey with his banner before him, for he had great desire to be the first that should enter the town, and he said to the knights that were about him, "Without this Lombard open the gate shortly we are like to die here for cold." "In the name of God, sir," said Pepin de Werre, "Lombards are malicious people and subtle; he is now looking on your crowns to see if they be all good or not, and to reckon if he have his whole sum or no." Therewith the king of England and the prince, his son, were ready at the gate, under the banner of sir Walter of Manny. Then the great gate was set open, and they all issued out. When the Frenchmen saw them issue and heard them cry, "Manny to the rescue!" they knew well they were betrayed. Then sir Geoffrey said to his company, "Sirs, if we fly we are clean lost, so it were better to fight with a good heart." The Englishmen heard these words and said, "By Saint George, ye say truly, shame have he that flieth." The Frenchmen alighted afoot and put their horses from them and ordered themselves in battle. When the king saw that, he stood still and said, "Let us order ourselves in battle, for our enemies will abide us." . . . .

Now let us speak of the king who was there unknown of his enemies, under the banner of sir Walter of Manny, and was afoot among his men to seek his enemies, who stood together with their spears, a five foot long. At the first meeting there was a sore rencontre; and the king lighted on the lord Eustace of Ribeaumont, who was a strong and hardy knight. There was a long fight between him and the king, that it was joy to behold them; at last they were put asunder, for a great company of both parties came the same way, and fought there fiercely together. The Frenchmen did there right valiantly, but especially the lord Eustace of Ribeaumont, who struck the king the same day two times on his knees, but finally the king himself took him prisoner, and so he yielded his sword to the king and said, "Sir knight, I yield me as your prisoner," for he knew not then that it was the king." And so the day was for the king of England, and all that were there with sir Geoffrey slain or taken.

1350.—Of a chaplet of pearls that the king of England gave to sir Eustace of Ribeaumont.

Froissart, ch. 152 (I. § 320).   *Jehan le Bel*, ch. 93.

When this battle was done the king returned again

to the castle of Calais, and caused all the prisoners to be brought thither. Then the Frenchmen knew well that the king had been there personally himself, under the banner of sir Walter of Manny. The king said he would give them all that night a supper in the castle of Calais; the hour of supper came and the tables were covered. And the king and his knights were there ready, every man in new apparel, and the Frenchmen also were there and made good cheer though they were prisoners. The king sat down, and the lords and knights about him, right honourably. The prince, the lords, and the knights of England served the king at the first mess; and at the second they sat down at another table; they were all well served and at great leizure. Then when supper was done and the tables taken away, the king tarried still in the hall with his knights, and with the Frenchmen, and he was bare headed saving a chaplet of fine pearls that he wore on his head. Then the king went from one to another of the Frenchmen. And when he came to sir Geoffrey of Charny, a little he changed his countenance, and looked on him and said, " Sir Geoffrey, by reason I should love you but a little, since you would steal by night from me that thing which I have so dearly bought, and which hath cost me so much gold. I am right joyous and glad that I have taken you with the proof. You would have a better market than I have had when you thought to have had Calais for twenty thousand crowns; but God hath holpen me, and you have failed of your purpose."

And therewith the king went from him, and he gave never a word to answer. Then the king came to sir Eustace of Ribeaumont and joyously to him he said, "Sir Eustace, you are the knight in the world that I have seen most valiantly assail his enemies and defend himself, and I never found knight that ever gave me so much ado, body to body, as you have done this day. Wherefore I give you the prize above all the knights of my court by right sentence." Then the king took the chaplet that was upon his head, being both fair, goodly, and rich, and said: "Sir Eustace, I give you this chaplet for the best doer in arms in the battle past of either party, and I desire you to bear it this year for the love of me. I know well you are fresh and amorous, and oftentimes are among ladies and damsels; say, wheresoever you come, that I did give it you. And I quit you from your prison and ransom, and you shall depart to-morrow if it please you."

1350, Aug.—Of the naval battle and slaughter of the Spaniards upon the sea near Winchelsea.

Avesbury, 184.

(Contests between Biscayan and English fleets, due largely to trade rivalries, had made the Channel unsafe; after this defeat, the Biscay towns agreed to a twenty years' peace).

Our lord the king, considering how that about the festival of All Saints a Spanish fleet, coming from the sea towards Bordeaux, had captured in the mouth of the Garonne several English ships laden with wine to carry to England, and had killed all the English they found on board, determined to punish them with a like penalty, and frighten them from putting their hands any more to such crimes ; and so on the day of the Beheading of St. John the Baptist, in the year of our Lord 1350, the twenty-fourth year of his reign in England and the eleventh of his reign in France, having brought together a sufficient fleet at Sandwich, with many nobles, men-of-arms, and archers on board, he joined battle on the sea, near Winchelsea, with the Spaniards, who were sailing home with many war-ships from Flanders, and purposing to ravage the English shores. They fought bravely, but he overcame them ; and very many of the Spaniards in the twenty-four great galleys perished by the sword or flying arrow ; and all the twenty-four galleys, laden with much merchandise, especially various sorts of cloth bought in Flanders, were captured. But some, with wares in other ships, kept aloof from the battle and escaped, for none pursued them.

1351.—Of the coinage of groats and half-groats.

Walsingham, i. 275. *Murimuth, Continuatio*, 182.

In the year of grace one thousand three hundred and fifty-one, which was the twenty-fifth year of the reign of king Edward, from the conquest the third, William of Edyngdon, bishop of Winchester, treasurer of the kingdom, and a man of great prudence, who loved the good of the king more than that of the community, devised and caused to be coined a new money, namely the groat and half-groat; but these were of less weight than the like sum of sterling. This was afterwards the cause that food and merchandise became dearer throughout the whole of England. Workmen, craftsmen, and servants became accordingly more cunning and fraudulent than ever. To provide against their cunning and pride, wickedness and avarice, statutes were afterwards ordained by the parliament at Westminster in the 28th and 35th years of the reign of Edward the third from the conquest; but they were of little or no service to the Commons.

1351, Feb.—Statute of Provisors.

25 *Edw. III., Statute* 4. *(Statutes of the Realm,* ed. 1810, i. 316.*)*

(This most important statute was an attempt to put an end to the papal encroachments on free election to bishoprics, and on private rights of patronage. In spite of frequent evasions, it had the effect of lessening the evil complained of.)

. . . . Now it is shewed to our lord the king in this present parliament holden at Westminster, at the Octave of the Purification of our Lady, the five-and-twentieth year of his reign of England and of France the twelfth, by the grievous complaints of all the commons of his realm, that the grievances and mischiefs aforesaid do daily abound, to the greater damage and destruction of all his realm of England, more than ever were before, viz., that now or late the bishop of Rome, by procurement of clerks or otherwise, hath reserved and doth daily reserve to his collation, generally and especially as well archbishopricks, bishopricks, abbeys and priories, as all other dignities and other benefices in England, which be of the advowry of* people of Holy Church, and give the same as well to aliens as to denizens, and taketh of all such benefices the first fruits, and many other profits; and a great part of the treasure of the said realm is carried away and dispended out of the realm, by the purchasers of such benefices and graces aforesaid; and also by such privy reservations many clerks advanced in this realm by their true patrons, which have peaceably holden their advancements by long time be suddenly put out; whereupon the said commons have prayed our said lord the king, that since the right of the crown of England and the law of the said realm is such that, upon the mischiefs and damages which happen to his realm, he ought and is bound by his oath, with the accord of his people in parliament, thereof to make remedy and law, in removing the mischiefs and damages which thereof ensue, it may please him thereupon to ordain remedy. Our lord the king . . . . . by the assent of all the great men and commonality of the said realm, to the honour of God and profit of the said Church of England and of all his realm hath ordered and established, that the free elections of archbishops, bishops, and all other dignities and benefices elective in England, shall hold from henceforth in the manner as they were granted by the king's progenitors, and the ancestors of other lords, founders of the said dignities and other

* In the gift of.

benefices. And that all prelates and other people of Holy Church, which have advowsons of any benefices of the king's gift, or of any of his progenitors, or of other lords and donors, to do divine services and other charges thereof ordained, shall have their collations and presentments freely to the same, in the manner as they were enfeoffed by their donors.

1352.—Statute of Treasons.

25 *Edward III. Stat.* 5, *c.* 2. (*Statutes of the Realm*, i. 319).

(This was the first definition by statute of the acts constituting treason, and it became the basis of all subsequent legislation and judicial decision.)

Item, whereas divers opinions have been before this time in what case treason shall be said and in what not; the king, at the request of the lords and of the commons, hath made a declaration in the manner as hereafter followeth, that is to say, when a man doth compass or imagine the death of our lord the king, or of our lady his queen, or of their eldest son and heir; or if a man do violate the king's consort, or the king's eldest daughter unmarried, or the wife of the king's eldest son and heir; or if a man do levy war against our lord the king in his realm, or be adherent to the king's enemies in his realm, giving to them aid and comfort in the realm or elsewhere, and thereof be proveably attainted of open deed by the people of their condition; and if a man counterfeit the king's great or privy seal or his money; and if a man bring false money into this realm counterfeit to the money of England, . . . knowing the money to be false, to merchandise or make payment in deceit of our said lord the king or of his people; and if a man slay the chancellor, treasurer, or the king's justices of the one bench or the other, justices in eyre or justices of assize, and all other justices assigned to hear or determine, being in their places, doing their offices. And it is to be understood that, in the cases above rehearsed, that ought to be judged treason which extends to our lord the king and his royal majesty; and of such treason the forfeiture of the escheats pertains to our sovereign lord, as well of the lands and tenements holden of others as of himself. And moreover there is another manner of treason, that is to say, when a servant slayeth his master or a wife her husband, or when a man secular or religious slayeth his prelate to whom he oweth faith and obedience; and of such treason the escheats ought to pertain to every lord of his own fee. And because that many like cases of treason may happen in time to come which a man cannot think nor declare at this present time, it is accorded that if any other case, supposed treason, which is not above specified, doth happen before any justices, the justices shall tarry without any going to judgment of the treason till the cause be showed before the king and his parliament, and it be declared whether it ought to be judged treason or other felony.

1353.—A statute against annullers of judgments of the king's court (commonly called the statute of Præmunire).

27 Edw. III., Stat. 1, *cap.* 1 (*Statutes*, i. 329).

(This, like the statute of Provisors, was a defensive measure against Rome, and was designed to prevent encroachments on the jurisdiction of the English courts. The act known later as the statute of Præmunire was a confirmation and completion of this, and was passed in 1393.)

Our lord the king, by the assent and prayer of the great men and the commons of the realm of England, at his great council holden at Westminster, the Monday next after the feast of Saint Matthew the Apostle, the twenty-seventh year of his reign of England, and of France the fourteenth, in amendment of his said realm, and maintenance of the laws and usages, hath ordained and stablished these things under written.

First, because it is shewed to our lord the king, by the grievous and clamorous complaints of the great men and commons aforesaid, how that divers of the people be and have been drawn out of the realm to answer of things, whereof the cognisance pertaineth to the king's court, and also that the judgments given in the same court be impeached in another court, in prejudice and disherison of our lord the king and of his crown and of all the people of his said realm and to the undoing and destruction of the common law of the same realm at all times used: whereupon, good deliberation had with the great men and others of his said council, it is assented and accorded by our lord the king and the great men and commons aforesaid, that all the people of the king's ligeance, of what condition they be, which shall draw any out of the realm in plea whereof the cognizance pertaineth to the king's court, or of things whereof judgments be given in the king's court, or which do sue in any other court, to defeat or impeach the judgments given in the king's court, shall have a day, containing the space of two months, by warning to be made to them in the place where the possessions be which be in debate, or otherwise where they have lands or other possessions, by the sheriffs or other the king's ministers, to appear before the king and his council, or in his chancery, or before the king's justices in his places of the one bench or the other, or before other the king's justices which to the same shall be deputed, to answer in their proper persons to the king of the contempt done in this behalf. And if they come not at the said day in their proper persons to be at the law, they, their procurators, attornies, executors, notaries, and maintainors shall from that day forth be put out of the king's protection, and their lands, goods, and chattels forfeit to the king, and their bodies, wheresoever they may be found, shall be taken and imprisoned, and ransomed at the king's will; and upon the same a writ shall be made to take them by their bodies, and to seize their lands, goods, and possessions, into the king's hands; and if it be returned, that they be not found, they shall be . . . . . . outlawed.

1351, March 27.—How the lord Robert of Beaumanoir went about to defy the captain of Ploërmel who had to name Bramborough, and how there was a sore battle of thirty against thirty.

Froissart (I. §§ 335-7).

(In spite of the truce between the English and French kings, the war continued in Brittany; Charles of Blois had been taken prisoner in 1347, and sent to join David Bruce in the Tower of London, but his wife gallantly continued the struggle. Its most celebrated episode was the Tourney of Ploërmel.)

In this same season there took place in Brittany a very great deed of arms that ought never to be forgotten, but rather ought to be put forward to encourage all young squires, and to give them an example. And that you may the better understand the matter you must know that there were wars continually between the parties of the two ladies Joan of Montfort and Joan of Blois, because that the lord Charles of Blois was imprisoned. And the parties of these same ladies warred on each other by means of their garrisons, which kept themselves within their castles and their strong towns both on the one side and on the other.

It chanced one day that the lord Robert of Beaumanoir, a right valiant knight and of the most high lineage in Brittany, who was seneschal of the castle which has to name the castle Josselin, and who had with him a goodly company of men-of-arms of his own lineage and others who were mercenaries, came before the town and the castle of Ploërmel. Its captain was a man named Bramborough, and he had with him a great company of mercenaries, German, English, and Breton, who were of the party of the countess of Montfort. And this same lord Robert with his company ran before the barriers, and would gladly have seen those within sally forth, but not one stirred. When sir Robert saw this, he approached yet a little nearer and called to the captain. And he came before the gate to speak with the said sir Robert, on the safe assurance on the one hand and on the other.

"Bramborough," said sir Robert, "are there no men of arms within your walls, either you or other two or three, who would joust with lances against other three on our party for the love of their friends?"

Bramborough answered and said, "Their friends would never wish that they should be evilly killed in a single joust, for that would be a chance of fortune too soon over, and would win them the name of foolhardiness and folly, rather than bring them renown. But I will tell you what we will do, an it please you. You shall take twenty or thirty of your companions from your garrison, and I will take as many from mine. And let us go to a fair field, where none shall hinder or trouble us, and command our companions, on pain of hanging, on the one side and on the other, and also all those who stand and watch us, that none shall give aid or comfort to any of the combatants. And there straitly in that place let us prove ourselves and do such things that in the time to come men shall speak of us in halls and in palaces, in public places and in all other parts of the world. And let the renown and the good-luck be to those to whom God shall award it."

"By my troth," said sir Robert of Beaumanoir, "I accord me thereunto, and right valiantly do you now speak. Therefore, be you thirty, and we also will be thirty, and this I vow on my faith."

"And this I also on my part vow," said Bramborough, "for there will thus be gained more honour, to him who there bears himself bravely than at a single joust."

Thus was the matter settled and sworn to; and the day agreed on was the Wednesday following. In the meantime each one chose those thirty followers that seemed good to him, and all these sixty looked well to their armour that all might be right and in good order.

When the day came Bramborough's thirty companions heard mass; then armed themselves and went to the place where the battle was to be, and there alighted on foot; and they straitly forbad all those who were there that they should come between them for whatever chance or peril they might see befall to their companions. And thus likewise did the thirty companions of the lord Robert of Beaumanoir. And these thirty companions, that we call the English, awaited for a great space those others that we call the French. When the thirty Frenchmen were come, they alighted from their horses and gave to their followers the same commandment that the English knights had given. Each side agreed that five of them should remain on horseback at the entrance of the place, and that the other twenty-five should alight. And when they were each before the other, the whole sixty held parley together for a short space ; then they drew back on the one side and on the other, and made all their followers withdraw to a greater distance. Then one of them made a sign, and forthwith they ran forward, and fiercely they fought in the press, and nobly they succoured each the other, where they saw their companions in great straits. And shortly after that they were gathered together, was one of the French party slain, but for all that the others never ceased the battle, but bore themselves as valiantly on the one part and on the other, as if they all had been Rolands and Olivers. I cannot say of a truth that they on this hand maintained themselves the better, or that they on that hand achieved greater things, nor have I heard either party prized before the other ; but they fought so long that one and all lost strength and breath and power altogether. And they were forced to stop and take rest ; and by agreement they rested, the one on this side and the other on that, and made truce until such time as they should be rested, and the first to arise was to call on the other party.

And of the Frenchmen there were slain four, and of the Englishmen two. Thus they rested on both sides for a long space, and drank wine that was brought to them in bottles, rebuckled their disordered armour, and dressed their wounds. When they were thus refreshed, the first party which arose made a sign and called on the other. Then began as before a sore and fierce battle which lasted a long while. They fought with the short swords of Bordeaux, strong and sharp, and with lances and daggers, and others with axes, and they gave each other marvellous great blows, and one and all threw themselves into the battle, and smote each other without sparing. You may well believe they did right noble deeds of arms man for man, body to body, and hand to hand. There has never been heard tell of such deeds for this hundred years past. Thus they fought together like good champions, and maintained this second encounter right valiantly, but finally the English were worsted. For thus have I heard it related how that one of the Frenchmen who was on horseback broke and scattered them so fiercely that Bramborough, their captain, and eight of their companions were there slain ; and the others yielded themselves prisoners when they saw how their defence would not aid them, for they could not and would not fly. And the same lord Robert and his companions who were yet alive took them, and led them to the castle Josselin as their prisoners, and afterwards put them to ransom courteously when that they were all cured of their hurts ; for there were none who were not sore wounded, Frenchmen no less than Englishmen.

And since that time I have seen sitting at the table of Charles king of France a Breton knight, sir Evan of Charuel who had been there ; and he had his face so cut about and hacked that it plainly showed how that the encounter had been nobly fought. And in many places was this adventure related and recorded, and some thought it prowess and others foolhardiness.

1351.—The Tourney of Ploërmel.

Translated from a French poem of the 14th century; in Buchon, Froissart, xiv., 303 (Coll. des Chronique, xxiv.)

Oh! hearken to my tale, ye lords and knights of chivalry,
Both bannerets and bachelors and men of high degree,
Let abbots eke and bishops hear and men of holy mind,
Heralds and wandering minstrels, and all companions kind,
Gentle and simple folk, in whatsoever land ye dwell,
Give heed unto this brave romance, that we to you would tell.
True is the tale and worthy, right worthy to be told,
How thirty English champions in war like lions bold,
Fought on a day with thirty knights of Breton lineage.

. . . .

Ere that the lord Dagorne was dead and knew this life no more,
(At Auril fell the baron the castle walls before,
—— On all such lords of Brittany and their companions brave
May our just God have mercy who knows to sain and save!

While yet this lord was living, he did all folk to know,
That no more should the village folk, the men who reap and sow,
Be captured of the Englishmen, and vexed with spear and sword ;
But, when he died, his comrades heeded no more his word,
For Bramborough clave unto him, to his allegiance true,
And by St. Thomas swore he a vengeful deed to do.
The Breton folk he harried and took the country side,
And Poetinel he plundered till her folk for pity cried.
All through the coasts of Brittany he wrought his evil way,
Up to the time that God had doomed to be his closing day ;
But at last the good lord Beaumanoir, whom all men loved to name,
The wise lord John of Beaumanoir, whose valour wrought him fame,
To parley with the Englishmen in happy hour he went,
And saw their wretched captives, and 'gan their woe lament.
For one was vexed with fetters, and another dragged a chain,
And another in the stocks was bound, and some were pent in pain,
And all were bound together with thongs in twos and threes,

Like to the cows and oxen men barter as they please.
When Beaumanoir beheld them, deep in his heart he sighed,
And unto Bramborough spake he, right noble in his pride;
"Oh knights of English chivalry, to right ye do foul scorn
In harrying the husbandmen, the men who sow the corn,
Who win for us our meat and wine where they themselves did sow.
Ah, had we not the husbandmen, too well we soon should know
The toil of working in the field, all noble though we be,
The work of threshing, hoeing, and bearing poverty.
To men unused like us to this no little toil it were.
Let these then rest henceforward, who have too much to bear,
Nor let the will of brave Dagorne be cast aside so soon."

(A combat is agreed upon, as described by Froissart in the previous extract.)

Now will I tell of Bramborough and all the deeds he wrought,
His thirty men he gathered, and them hath fairly brought
Straight to the field appointed, in gallant wise and gay,
And then to all his company these noble truths 'gan say,
"Well have I conned my magic, my books of mystery,
And on this day doth Merlin foretell us victory.

Henceforth o'er France and Brittany, if I the truth
    can know,
Shall Edward have the governance; for fate will
    have it so."

   .   .   .   .   .   .

Then spake he unto Beaumanoir, "Look not for
    ruth from me;
My mind is fixed before my love this day to carry
    thee.
This day I vow to lead thee a captive to her bower."
And Beaumanoir cried back to him, "Deemest thou
    that will is power?
Lo! I and all my company know our intent aright,
And if the Lord of Glory aid and Mary lend us
    might,
If good St. Yvës help us, in whom our trust we place,
Mock not thyself with idle hopes, but cast the die
    apace.
The hazard is against thee, and short thy life shall be."
And Alain, lord of Carromois, heard too, and loud
    cried he,
"Bramboro', thou villain traitor! hop'st thou that
    this shall be?
Think'st thou that men like Beaumanoir can yield
    to men like thee?
For him upon my body forthwith I thee defy,
And now before my edged blade I deem that thou
    shalt die."
Straightway the lord of Carromois hath smitten him
    with might

And sorely stabbed him with his lance, the spearhead
    keen and bright,
Right through his face the spearhead went, for all
    men round to see,
And right within his brain-pan stuck and pierced
    him grievously.
Then Alain thrust the spear from him and laid bold
    Bramborough low;
But Bramborough leapt to gain his feet and thought
    to reach his foe,
Then Geoffrey lord of Borës dealt him a blow amain
And pierced him with his spearhead and laid him
    low again,
Till in the dust bold Bramborough fell with a crash
    and died.
Then to the lord of Beaumanoir brave Geoffrey gladly
    cried,
"Where art thou? see'st this vengeance? see'st thou
    who here lies slain?"
And Beaumanoir hath heard him and answered back
    again,
"Now 'tis the time for prowess! on to the combat
    go!
On, lords, to war with others and leave the dead man
    low."
Then well saw all the Englishmen, how Bramborough
    there was dead,
And all their pride fell from them, and all their
    boasting fled.
Then to his friends cried Croucart, a German fell
    in fight,

"Lords, wot ye well the truth this day and know
    your case aright,
Bramborough, who led us hither with bitter mockery,
Has mocked us, and his trusted books of Merlin's
    mystery
Have not been worth a penny to him for all his trust.
Dead on his back with gaping throat he lieth in the
    dust.
Now act we all like wise men, like comrades brave
    and stout,
Stand back to back in order close, and fight the
    battle out.
Let all who come against us find death or sudden
    fear."

   .   .   .   .

Then fiercely went the battle and victory came slow,
As still the dreadful combat went swaying to and fro.

   .   .   .   .

And hot the sun shone over them, and every man did
    sweat,
With sweat and blood beneath their feet the earth
    itself grew wet.
It chanced on this fair Saturday that Beaumanoir
    kept fast,
And evil grew his thirst to him; he cried for drink
    at last,
And Geoffrey, lord of Borës, heard him, and answered
    "Nay,
Drink of thy blood, lord Beaumanoir, thy thirst
    thyself canst stay.

This day we win great glory, no man shall lack his
    fame ;
Our great renown of valour shall never bring us
    blame."
Then did the lord of Beaumanoir take courage and
    delight,
And all his thirst passed from him in the joy and
    breath of fight.
And from each side the battles met fiercely face to
    face,
And men fell dead or wounded ; few living left that
    place.

1354.—How the duke of Lancaster in vain treated for peace at Avignon.

Knighton, 2607.

(Philip VI. of France had died in 1350, and his eldest son John had succeeded him. In spite of the war in Brittany, the truce was several times renewed ; and in 1354 the new pope, Innocent VI., seemed likely to bring about peace. A conference of ambassadors met at Guines near Calais, and Edward offered to give up his claim to the French throne if Guienne were given him in full sovereignty. The treaty was to be completed at Avignon.)

Then were sent to Avignon to the pope to treat for peace the duke of Lancaster, the earl of Arundel, the bishop of Norwich, and many magnates. But the ambassadors of France, to wit the duke of Bourbon, the earl of Armagnac, and the rest, disavowed all the articles to which they had consented and agreed at Calais, and would accept no peace except on their own terms, declaring that they were ready and able to defend their land against the English, world without end; and so they parted. For the French demanded, first, that the king of England should give up the arms of France; secondly, that the king of England should do homage to the king of France for Gascony. The duke of Lancaster replied that the arms of France, which he bore by the counsel of his liege men of France, he would not give up for any man living. Also the king of England would not do homage to a man to whom he claimed to be superior by hereditary right from his mother. But if they would propose any other reasonable terms of peace, the king of England loved peace so much that he would accept them.

Henry duke of Lancaster, having with him the the earl of Arundel and the rest, had arrived at Avignon on Christmas Eve, with two hundred horses, of which thirty-two were covered with harness of mail, and he remained there for six weeks with great honour. Indeed, when he had been approaching the city, bishops, nobles, citizens, and commons had come out to meet him to the number of two thousand horsemen; and there was such a crowd that from the third hour of the day to vespers they could scarce pass over the city bridge. When he had entered the city, he had gone straightway to the palace of the pope. And, arriving there, he dismounted and, entering in, saluted the pope with due reverence, as he knew well how to do, and, after brief converse, passed to his lodging. The joys of feasting and drinking were always ready, so long as he stayed there, for all who wished to come and refresh themselves; and everything was so carefully provided that all the court was astonished; —before his arrival, a hundred casks of wine had been got ready in his cellar. He showed such courtesy to all, especially to the pope and the cardinals, that they said the wide world had not his fellow. After he had left the papal court, the French laid ambush for him to take him, but by the help of God he escaped many snares and came to England with great honour.

1354.—Of the trouble between the Oxford scholars and laity.

Avesbury, 197.

On the festival of S. Scolastica the Virgin a quarrel began in a tavern at Oxford between a scholar and the taverner about a quart of wine, and the scholar after pouring the wine over the taverner broke his head with the quart pot. Whereupon there arose a great conflict between the scholars of the university and the laymen of the town of Oxford, in which many laymen were wounded and about twenty were slain; and some of the scholars also were severely wounded; and this conflict went on at intervals for two days. On the second day the monks made a solemn procession supplicating for peace. But still the conflict went on; and a young scholar pursued by laymen ran for safety to a monk who was with due humility bearing the Body of Christ in the procession, hoping that he would be saved by their reverence for the Body; but in vain, for the laymen cruelly attacked the innocent youth and mortally wounded him. Later in the same day the riot stopped, by the grace of God, and peace was publicly proclaimed between the parties. But next morning the laymen from the villages around Oxford, confederate with the laymen of that town, came in hostile array and great power into the town of Oxford with a black banner before them. They drove the scholars to their inns, broke about twenty doors of scholars' houses, went into the private rooms in the inns and killed, so it was said, many scholars, cut their books about with knives and axes, and carried off much of their property. Thus, alas! the university was dissolved, and no one became bachelor or master in dialectic art; all the scholars went home, except only the scholars of Merton Hall and of other like halls, and a few others.

On the first Sunday in Lent the king held a great feast and made a great tournament at Woodstock, because just then the queen was churched after the birth of her son Thomas, who was born there, and was held over the sacred font by Thomas, bishop of Durham. The bishop of Lincoln receiving full information of the troubles at Oxford, inhibited all the rectors and other priests over the whole of Oxford from celebrating mass or other divine offices in the presence of any layman of the town; and this interdict was not removed for more than a year. The king also sent his justices to the town, and many laymen and clergy also were conducted before them. Four of the more important burgesses of the town were indicted, and by royal command arrested, and taken off to the Tower of London, and there remained in prison. And in the great council held at Westminster after Easter, in the year 1355, our lord the king took into his hands the whole quarrel between the scholars and laity of Oxford, and, saving all rights, pardoned certain scholars for all the faults they had committed, and gave orders by writs to all the sheriffs of England that this should be publicly proclaimed; and accordingly in summer the university of Oxford flourished again in all the faculties. For some took their degrees in the dialectic art, some in theology, some in civil law, some in canon law, and some in both civil and canon. And our lord the king granted the complete supervision of the assize of bread, ale, and wine, and all victuals to the chancellor of the university, excluding the mayor entirely. The corporation paid as a fine to the university two hundred and fifty pounds sterling, without detriment to individual suits.

1355.—How the prince of Wales crossed to Gascony.
Avesbury, 201.

It was determined in the council at Westminster that the lord Edward, the prince of Wales, who was in the 24th year of his age, should cross to Gascony, and should have with him the earls of Warwick, Suffolk, Salisbury, and Oxford, with a thousand men of arms, two thousand archers, and a great number of Welsh. Soon afterwards the prince journeyed from London to Plymouth, where the navy for the passage was gathering, and there stayed, because the winds were contrary, until the festival of the Nativity of the Blessed Mary; and then the prince, with some three hundred ships and many more men than had been ordained, set sail with a favorable wind from the north, and safely and quickly passed to Gascony, where he was received by the Gascons with great joy, and there performed great deeds, as will appear later.

SEAL OF THE BLACK PRINCE.

1355.—How the duke of Lancaster tarried on the sea, and of the treason plotted by the king of Navarre.

Avesbury, 202.

At the same time the king of England caused his forty great ships to be prepared at Rotherhithe in the Thames with food for a quarter of a year; each of these vessels bore the banners of the lord Henry duke of Lancaster, and were filled with picked men at arms and archers; but they took no horses with them. The whole was commanded by the said duke, and he had with him two sons of the king, namely, the lord Lionel of Antwerp and John of Gaunt, the elder being then sixteen, as well as the earls of Northampton, of March, and of Stafford. On the tenth of July they began to sail and got to Greenwich. There and at Sandwich they tarried until the festival of the Assumption, the wind being constantly from the west or the east, so that they could not sail. With difficulty they got as far as Winchelsey, and afterwards to the Isle of Wight. Meanwhile the king was on board with the duke, in order to negotiate with the ambassadors of the king of Navarre,* who frequently came across to him. The fleet were in this condition when it was rumoured that the duke intended to cross to Normandy, where the king of Navarre promised to receive him in his castle of Cherbourg. For a quarrel had arisen between the king of Navarre and John king of France, wherefore the former turned from John, and sent promises to the king of England that he would join him with all his power. But bye-and-bye the duke of Lancaster learnt through spies that the king of Navarre had made peace with the king of France, and that the latter plotted to entrap the king of England and

* See *Appendix*.

the duke. And this was proved by the evidence of fact.

For near the castle on the sea coast there lay in ambush several thousand men of arms, some French and others German mercenaries, awaiting the duke's arrival. So when he heard of the treachery which was thus plotted, the duke, since his force was small in comparison with the enemy, and he had no cavalry, returned into England, his plan having been frustrated completely.

1355.—How the king of England crossed to Calais and laid waste a great part of Picardy.

Avesbury, 204.

On the Saturday after the feast of the Nativity of the Blessed Virgin Mary, the king caused proclamation to be made in the city of London that all nobles, men of arms, and archers should be ready at Sandwich on S. Michael's day, to cross with him to Calais. For he had heard that king John of France had prepared a great army to fight with him as soon as he should come into those parts. So about that time the lord Thomas, bishop of Durham, the lord of Percy, and the other nobles of the north, made a truce with the Scots to last till the day of the Nativity of S. John next following; and then the said lords came to the king at Sandwich, and crossed with him. The king had with him his two sons, the lord Lionel of Antwerp, and the lord John of Ghent, as well as the lord Henry Duke of Lancaster, and the earls of Northampton, March, and Stafford. At Calais also he found a thousand good men of arms, mercenaries from Flanders, Brabant, and Germany. And the Londoners had sent to the king twenty-five men of arms, and a body of five hundred archers, at their own expense. So altogether the king had more than three thousand men of arms, a great number of armed men, about two thousand mounted archers, as well as very many archers on foot. On the second of November the king left Calais with his army, and marched towards St. Omer, laying waste all the country as he passed. When John king of France, who was near St. Omer with a strong army, heard this he sent a certain knight, named sir Boucicault,—who had been captured in Gascony and had long been a prisoner in the hands of the king of England, but had just been ransomed,—to speak with the king of England and observe his army. And when he met the king, and with his permission had observed the three divisions of the English so nobly ordered, and composed of such warlike and wonderfully brave men, he was surprised that the king of England had such a large force with him, considering that the prince of Wales had also so great an army in Gascony. So he returned to king John and told him what he had seen. Then king John was sore troubled, and feared to meet the noble king of England face to face, but rather sought subterfuges; and therefore turned round and marched off, as far in front of the king of England as he could, destroying all provisions on the way that the English should not use them. The king of England pursued the retreating foe for some days, finding however very little food; and the scarcity of drink was such that for three days the greater part of the English army had nothing to drink but water. And when the king had passed Hesdin towards Amiens, seeing the cowardice of the enemy, and that they would not give battle. . . he returned through more fruitful lands to Boulogne, and thence returned to Calais, having been away ten days. Next day the constable of France and other Frenchmen came to Calais and offered battle for the next Tuesday. To whom the English lords replied at the order of the king, that the king wanted as much as possible to avoid the shedding of Christian blood, and therefore wished to meet his adversary, body to body, in his own cause, on condition that their right to the kingdom of France should be decided by battle between the two alone; or if his adversary was unwilling to fight by himself, then each should add to himself his eldest son; and if this were not enough, each should take two, three, or four noble knights nearest in blood to themselves and their sons; and that the conquered should yield his claims to the conqueror. These offers the Frenchmen totally rejected, and promised battle on the Tuesday.

(The Frenchmen would not accept an earlier day, nor pledge themselves to the good faith of John : Tuesday was at last agreed upon, but John did not appear).

Whereupon Edward gave each of the foreign mercenaries over, and above the promised pay, presents in proportion to their rank, and returned to England much praised.

1355.—Capture of Berwick by the Scots.

Avesbury, 209-10.

(In 1354 the conditions upon which king David Bruce should be free had been arranged, but before they could be carried out, French men and money appeared in Scotland and encouraged the national party to renew the struggle.)

While the events above told were taking place abroad, the Scots came secretly to the town of Berwick with great force, on the sixth of November, and entered the town at sunrise by stealth and unobserved by the garrison. Two or three English who tried to resist were slain; the whole town and all that it contained were captured; save that some took refuge in the castle and held it.

(Edward on his return held a parliament, which granted him large supplies.)

On S. Andrew's day (Nov. 30), parliament being at an end, our noble lord the king hastened towards Scotland, and kept Christmas at Newcastle-on-Tyne; meanwhile causing a great army to be gathered for the recovery of Berwick.

1355.—Of the terrible and wonderful expedition of the prince of Wales from Bordeaux to Narbonne.

Avesbury, 210.

While the king of England was in Northumberland preparing to enter Scotland, letters came to London from the lord Edward, his eldest son, who was then warring in Gascony, and also other letters from the lord John of Wingfield, knight, who was then and had long been as it were the leader and chief councillor of the prince, directed to the lord bishop of Winchester, treasurer of the king, saying how the prince had harried all the lands not yet under the allegiance of the king of England from the city of Bordeaux to the city of Narbonne, which is near the Greek sea.* He had taken by assault about five hundred country towns, and many great cities and walled towns, taking infinite spoil, and laying the country waste by fire for eight weeks. The city of Narbonne was captured, all but the castle; and when the men of Montpellier heard this, they feared lest they should suffer the same fate, and therefore had all the houses in the suburbs taken down and the materials carried into the city. The scholars of the university there, and even the friars, and many others who lived in the suburbs, as well as a great number from the country around, betook themselves in terror to Avignon, with such property as they could carry, that they might be under the protection of the pope. Our lord the pope, not thinking himself safe, caused all the gates of his palace to be secured with iron. The pope's marshal went out to meet the prince with more than five hundred men of arms, some Provençals and some from the retinues of the lord cardinals, but fifty of his men were slain, the marshal himself was captured, and set to ransom for 50,000 shield-florins, bringing back scarcely more than 80 of his men. *So they were shrunk in the wetting!* After destroying Narbonne, the prince of Wales heard that the earl of Armagnac, the constable of France, the marshal of Clermont,

* The Mediterranean.

and the prince of Orange, with other magnates, had gathered an innumerable force against him, and were coming against him to join battle, and therefore he turned to meet them. Whereupon the Frenchmen were struck with terror, and dared not to stand in his way, and fled into the mountains and other safe places where they could not be attacked.

1356.—Burnt Candlemas.

Avesbury, 235.

(The Scotch in Berwick had quickly capitulated. Edward now thought it possible to gain the direct sovereignty of Scotland, and caused Edward Balliol to formally make over to him all his rights to the throne.)

On Jan. 27 the lord Edward, king of England, the kingdom and crown of Scotland having been thus transferred to him at Roxburgh, began to ride forward in his new kingdom of Scotland, having with him three thousand men of arms, and ten thousand armed men, more than ten thousand archers on horseback, and as many more on foot, carrying among other standards the royal banner of Scotland. Then William Douglas, a lord very rich in those parts, came to the king with words of peace, and craftily begged for a truce of ten days, wherein he might speak to the other nobles of the kingdom of Scotland, and win them over to the allegiance of the new king of Scotland. And the king, being perfect in charity and believing everything, granted him the truce. But, during the ten days, the said William and the other lords of those parts around the Scotch sea had as much of their property as they could carried to the castles and other secret subterranean places, and then when the ten days were over, they fled from the face of the king and betook themselves to hiding-places in the woods and marshes. Then the king, seeing that he was greatly deceived by William Douglas, ravaged aud burnt all his lands and those of other lords as far as the Scotch sea, so that nothing that could be taken remained unburnt. But they had very little food, and many ships coming from England to the king with food were so horribly tost by the tempests of the sea that some of them were lost, others were driven by the winds to various English ports, and some were borne to foreign parts. So, as food failed them, our lord the king returned to England, being for the time frustrated in his purpose.

1356.—The night before Poitiers.

Froissart, ch. 159 (1. § 377.)

(In the summer the duke of Lancaster crossed to La Hogue, and ravaged Normandy; but being met by the French king with a superior force he turned aside into Brittany. On July 6, the prince of Wales left Bordeaux with a small army and marched north, hoping to join Lancaster. King John thereupon turned south and near Poitiers caught up the prince who was returning on account of failure of provisions.)

. . . Thus the prince rode that Saturday from the morning till it was against night, so that he came within two little leagues of Poitiers; then the Captal de Buch, sir Aymenon of Pumiers, the lord Bartholomew of Berghersh, and lord Eustace d'Ambreticourt, all these the Prince sent forth, to see if they might know what the Frenchmen did. These knights departed with two hundred men of arms well horsed. They rode so far that they saw the great host of the king of France; they saw all the fields covered with men of arms. These Englishmen could not forbear, but set on the tail of the French host, and cut down many to the earth, and took divers prisoners; so that the host began to stir and tidings thereof came to the French king as he was entering into the city of Poitiers. Then he returned again, and made all his host do the same, so that Saturday it was very late ere he was lodged in the field. The English scouts returned again to the prince and shewed him all that they saw and knew, and said how the French host was a great number of people. "Well," said the prince, "in the name of God let us now study how we shall fight with them to our advantage." That night the Englishmen lodged in a strong place among hedges, vines, and bushes; and their host was well watched, and so was the French host.

1356. Of the order of the French before the battle of Poitiers.

Froissart ch. 160 (I. § 378).

On the Sunday in the morning the French king, who had great desire to fight with the Englishmen, heard his mass in his pavilion, and was houseled and his four sons with him. After mass there came to him the duke of Orleans, the duke of Bourbon, the count of Ponthieu . . . . and divers others;

all these with the king went to council. Then finally it was ordained that all manner of men should draw into the field, and every lord display his banner and set forth in the name of God and saint Denis. Then trumpets blew up through the host, and every man mounted on horseback and went into the field, where they saw the king's banner wave with the wind. There might have been seen great nobles with fair harness and rich array of banners and pennons, for there was all the flower of France. There was none durst abide at home without he would be shamed for ever. Then it was ordained by the advice of the constable and marshals that three lines of battle should be made ; and in each division sixteen thousand men of arms. . . . The first battle the duke of Orleans was to govern with thirty-six banners and twice as many pennons; the second the duke of Normandy and his two brethren the lord Louis and the lord John; the third the king himself. And while these battles were setting in array, the king called to him the lord Eustace Ribeaumont, the lord John of Landas and the lord Guiscard of Beaujeu, and said to them, "Sirs, ride on before to see the dealing of the Englishmen, and mark well what number they be, and by what means we may fight with them, either on foot or a horseback." These three knights rode forth. The king was on a white charger and cried aloud to his men, "Sirs, among you when you are at Paris,.at Chartres, at Rouen, or at Orleans, then you do threaten the Englishmen and desire to be in arms out against them. Now you are come thereto; I shall now shew you them; now shew forth your evil will that ye bear them, and make them to rue the displeasures and damages they have done you, for without doubt we shall fight with them." Such as heard him said, " Sir, in God's name so be it; that would we see gladly." Herewith the three knights returned again to the king, who demanded of them tidings. Then sir Eustace of Ribeaumont answered for all, and said, " Sir, we have seen the Englishmen, and, by estimation, they are two thousand men at arms, and four thousand archers, and fifteen hundred others; howbeit they are in a strong place. And, as far as we can imagine, they are arranged in one body; howbeit they are wisely ordered, and along the way they have fortified strongly the hedges and bushes; one part of their archers are along by the hedge, so that none can go nor ride that way but must pass by them. And that way must you go, if you purpose to fight with them. In this hedge there is but one entry and one issue, through which perchance but four horsemen may ride abreast; at the end of this hedge, where no man can go nor ride, there be men of arms afoot and archers before them in manner of a harrow, so that they will not be lightly discomfited." " Well," said the king, " what will you then counsel us to do?" Sir Eustace said, " Sir, let us all be afoot except three hundred men of arms well horsed, of the best in your host and most hardy, to the intent they may somewhat break and open the archers; and then your divisions to follow on quickly afoot, and so to fight with their men of arms hand to hand. This is the best advice that I can give you; if any other think any other way better, let him speak." The king said, "Thus shall it be done."

1356.—How the cardinal of Périgord treated to make agreement between the French king and the prince before the battle of Poitiers.

Froissart, ch. 161 (I. § 380.)

When the French king's lines of battle were ordered and every lord under his banner among his own men, then it was commanded that every man should cut his spear to five feet long, and every man put off his spurs. Thus as they were ready to approach, the cardinal of Périgord came in great haste to the king; he came the same morning from Poitiers; he kneeled down to the king and held up his hands, and desired him for God's sake a little to abstain setting forward till he had spoken with him. Then he said, "Sir, ye have here all the flower of your realm against a handful of Englishmen in comparison to your company. And, sir, if you may have them accorded to you without battle, it shall be more profitable and honourable to have them by that manner, rather than to adventure so noble chivalry as you have here present. Sir, I beg of you in the name of God and humility that I may ride to the prince, and shew him what danger you have him in." The king said, "It pleaseth me well; but return again shortly." The cardinal departed, and diligently he rode to the prince, who was among his men afoot. Then the cardinal alighted, and came to the prince, who received him courteously. Then the cardinal, after his salutation made, said, "Certainly, fair son, if you and your counsel consider rightly the puissance of the French king, you will suffer me to treat to make a peace between you, if I may." The prince, who was young and lusty, said, "Sir, the honour of me and of my people saved, I would gladly fall to any reasonable way."

Then the cardinal said, "Sir, you say well, and I shall accord you if I can; for it should be great pity if so many noble men and others as be here on both parties should come together by battle." . . . . . That Sunday all the day the cardinal travailed in riding from the one host to the other gladly to agree them. . . . . . In the meanseason that the cardinal rode thus between the hosts, in trust to do some good, certain knights of France and of England both rode forth the same Sunday, because it was truce for that day, to coast the hosts and to behold the dealing of their enemies. So it fortuned that the lord John Chandos rode the same day coasting the French host; and in like manner the lord of Clermont, one of the French marshals, had ridden forth and viewed the state of the English host; and as these two knights returned towards their hosts they met together, and each of them bore one manner of device; a blue lady embroidered in a sunbeam above on their apparel. Then the lord Clermont said : "Chandos, how long have you taken on you to bear my device?" "Nay, you bear mine," said Chandos, "for it is as well mine as yours." "I deny that," said Clermont, "and if it were not for the truce this day between us, I should make it good on you forthwith that you have no right to bear my device." "Ha! sir," said Chandos, "you shall find me to-morrow ready to meet you, and to prove by feat of arms that it is as well mine as yours." Then Clermont said, "Chandos, these be well the words of you Englishmen, for you can devise nothing new, but all that you see is good and fair." So they departed without any more doing, and each of them returned to their host.

The cardinal of Périgord could in no wise that Sunday make any agreement between the parties; and when it was near night he returned to Poitiers. . . . . . . All the prince's company passed not eight thousand men of one and other, and the Frenchmen were sixty thousand fighting men, whereof there were more than three thousand knights.

1356, Sept. 19.—Of the battle of Poitiers between the prince of Wales and the French king.

Froissart, ch. 162 (1. § 384).

When the prince saw that he should have battle, and that the cardinal was gone without any peace or truce making, and saw that the French king did not set but little store by him, he said then to his men, "Now, sirs, though we are but a

BATTLE OF POITIERS.

small company as in regard to the puissance of our enemies, let us not be abashed therefor, for the victory lieth not in the multitude of people, but where as God will send it. If it fortune that the day be ours, we shall be the most honoured people of all the world; and if we die in our right quarrel, I have the king my father and my brethren, and also you have good friends and kinsmen, these shall avenge us. Therefore, sirs, for God's sake I require you to do your devoir this day; for if God be pleased and Saint George, this day shall see me a good knight." These words and such others that the prince spake comforted all his people. The lord sir John Chandos that day never went from the prince: nor also the lord James Audley, for a great while; but when he saw that they should needs fight, he said to the prince, "Sir, I have served always truly my lord your father and you also, and shall do as long as I live; I say this because I made once a vow that the first battle that either the king your father or any of his children should be at, how that I would be one of the first setters-on, or else to die in the pain. Therefore, I require your grace as in regard for any service that ever I did to the king your father or to you, that you will give me licence to depart from you and to set myself there as I may accomplish my vow." The prince accorded to his desire and said, "Sir James, God give you this day that grace to be the best knight of all others," and so took him by the hand. Then the knight departed from the prince, and went to the foremost front of all the battles, only accompanied with four squires who promised not to fail him. This lord James was a right sage and a valiant knight, and by him was much of the host ordained and governed the day before. . . . . Then the battle began on all parts, and the lines of the marshals of France approached, and they set forth that were appointed to break the ranks of the archers. They entered a-horse-back into the way, where the great hedges were on both sides set full of archers. As soon as the men of arms entered, the archers began to shoot on both sides, and did slay and hurt horses and knights. So that the horses, when they felt the sharp arrows, would in no wise go forward, but drew back and flung and took on so fiercely that many of them fell on their masters, so that for press they could not rise again. Insomuch that the marshal's division could never come at the prince. Certain knights and squires that were well mounted passed through the archers, and thought to approach to the prince, but they could not. The lord James Audley, with four squires, was in the front of that battle, and there did marvels in arms; and by great prowess he came and fought with sir Arnold d'Andrehen under his own banner, and there they fought long together, and sir Arnold was there sore handled. The division of the marshals began to disorder by reason of the shot of the archers with the aid of the men of arms, who came in among

them, and slew them, and did what they list.
And there was the lord Arnold D'Andrehen taken
prisoner by other men than by sir James Audley, or
by his four squires, for that day he never took
prisoner, but always fought and went on his enemies.
Also, on the French part, the lord John Clermont
fought under his own banner as long as he could
endure; but there he was beaten down and could
not be relieved nor ransomed, but was slain without
mercy; some said it was because of the words that
he had the day before to sir John Chandos. So
within a short space the marshal's divisions were
discomfited, for they fell one upon another and
could not go forth; and the Frenchmen that were
behind and could not get forward recoiled back, and
came on the battalion of the duke of Normandy,
which was great and thick and afoot; but
anon they began to open behind. For when they
knew that the marshal's division was discomfited
they took their horses and departed, he that might
best. Also they saw a rout of Englishmen coming
down a little mountain on horseback and many
archers with them, who broke in on the side of the
duke of Orleans' division. True to say, the archers
did their company that day great advantage, for they
shot so thick that the Frenchmen wist not on what
side to take heed; and little and little the Englishmen won ground on them. And when the men of
arms of England saw that the marshal's division
was discomfited, and that the duke's division began to
disorder and open, they leapt then on their horses

which they had ready by them. Then they assembled together, and cried "Saint George for Guienne!" And the lord Chandos said to the prince, "Sir, take your horse and ride forth; this enterprise is yours; God is this day in your hands; get us to the French king's division, for there lieth all the sore of the matter. I think verily by his valiantness he will not fly; I trust we shall have him, by the grace of God and Saint George, so he be well fought withal. And sir, I heard you say that this day I should see you a good knight." The prince said, "Let us go forth; you shall not see me this day turn back." Then he said, "Advance banner in the name of God and of Saint George!" The knight that bore it did his commandment. There was then a sore battle and a perilous, and many a man overthrown; and he that was once down could not be raised again, without great succour and aid. As the prince rode and entered in among his enemies, he saw on his right hand, in a little bush lying dead, the lord Robert of Durazzo and his banner by him, and ten or twelve of his men about him. Then the prince said to two of his squires and to three archers, "Sirs, take the body of this knight on a shield and bear him to Poitiers, and present him from me to the Cardinal of Périgord and say how I salute him by this token." And this was done. The prince was informed that the cardinal's men were on the field against him, howbeit without the knowledge or consent of their master, the which was not according to the right order of arms; for men of the Church, that come and go for treaty of peace, ought not by reason to bear arms nor to fight for either of the parties; they ought to be indifferent. And because these men had done so, the prince was displeased with the cardinal, and therefore he sent unto him his nephew, the lord Robert of Durazzo, dead. . . . . .

The lord James Audley with the aid of his four squires fought always in the chief of the battle. He was sore hurt in the body and in the visage; as long as his breath served him, he fought. At last, at the end of the battle, his four squires took and brought him out of the field, and laid him under a hedge-side for to refresh him. And they unarmed him and bound up his wounds as well as they could. On the French part, king John was that day a full right good knight; if the fourth part of his men had done their devoirs as well as he did, the day had been his by all likelihood.

1356.—How king John was taken prisoner at the battle of Poitiers.

Froissart, ch. 163 (1. § 392).

Often times the adventures of love and of war are more fortunate and marvellous than any man can think or wish. Truly this battle, the which was near to Poitiers, in the fields of Beaumont and Maupertuis, was right great and perilous, and many deeds of arms there were done, the which came not all to knowledge. The fighters on both parties endured much pain. King John with his own hands did that day marvels in arms; he had an axe in his hands, wherewith he defended himself and fought in the breaking of the press. The chase endured to the gates of Poitiers; there were many slain and beaten down, horse and man, for they of Poitiers closed their gates and would suffer none to enter. Wherefore in the street before the gate was horrible murder, men hurt and beaten down. The Frenchmen yielded themselves as far off as they might know an Englishman; there were divers English archers that had four, five, or six prisoners. . . . . Then there was a great press to take the king, and such as knew him cried "Sir, yield you, or else you are but dead!" There was a knight of Saint Omer retained in wages with the king of England, called sir Denis Morbeque, who had served the Englishmen five years before, because in his youth he had forfeited the realm of France for a murder that he did at Saint Omer. It happened so well for him that he was next to the king when they were about to take him. He stept forth into the press, and by strength of his body and arms he came to the French king, and said in good French, "Sir, yield you." The king beheld the knight and said, "To whom shall I yield me? Where is my cousin the prince of Wales? If I might see him, I would speak with him." Denis answered and said, "Sir, he is not here, but yield you to me, and I shall bring you to him." "Who are you?" quoth the king. "Sir," quoth he, "I am Denis of Morbeque, a knight of Artois, but I

serve the king of England because I am banished
the realm of France, and I have forfeited all that
I had there." Then the king gave him his right
gauntlet, saying "I yield me to you." There was
a great press about the king, for every man was anxious
to say "I have taken him;" so that the king
could not go forward with his young son, the lord
Philip, with him by cause of the press. The prince
of Wales, who was courageous and cruel as a lion,
took that day great pleasure to fight and to chase his
enemies. The lord John Chandos who was with
him all that day never left him, and never took
heed of taking of any prisoner. Then, at end of the
battle, he said to the prince, "Sir, it were good that
you rested here, and set your banner ahigh in this
bush, that your people may draw hither, for they be
sore spread abroad; I can see no more banners
nor pennons of the French party. Wherefore, sir,
rest and refresh you, for you are sore chafed." Then
the prince's banner was set up ahigh on a bush, and
trumpets and clarions began to sound. Then the
prince did take off his basenet; and the knights for
his body and those of his chamber were ready about
him and a red pavilion pitched. And when the
two marshals were come to the prince he demanded
of them if they knew any tidings of the French king.
They answered and said, "Sir, we hear none of
certainty, but we think verily he is either dead or
taken, for he is not gone out of the battle." Then
the prince said to the earl of Warwick and to sir
Reynold Cobham, "Sirs, I require you to go forth

and see what you can know, that at your return you may show me the truth." These two lords took their horses and departed from the prince, and rode up a little hill to look about them. Then they perceived a flock of men of arms coming together right wearily. There was the French king afoot in great peril; for Englishmen and Gascons were his masters. They had taken him from sir Denis Morbeque perforce, and such as were most of force said, "I have taken him." "Nay," quoth another, "I have taken him;" so they strove which should have him. Then the French king to escape that peril said, "Sirs, strive not, lead me courteously and my son to my cousin the prince, and strive not for my taking. For I am a lord great enough to make you all rich." The king's words somewhat appeased them, howbeit ever as they went they made riot and brawled for the taking of the king. When the two aforesaid lords saw and heard that noise and strife among them, they came to them and said, "Sirs, what is the matter that you strive for?" "Sirs," said one of them, "it is for the French king, who is here taken prisoner; and there be more than ten knights and squires that challenge the taking of him and his son." Then the two lords entered into the press, and caused every man to draw aback, and commanded them in the prince's name, on pain of their heads, to make no more noise and to approach the king no nearer without they were commanded. Then every man gave room to the lords, and they alighted and did their reverence to the king, and so brought him and his son in peace and rest to the Prince of Wales.

1356.—How the prince made a supper to the French king the same day of the battle.

Froissart, ch. 168. (1. § 397.)

The same day of the battle at night the prince made a supper in his lodging to the French king and to the most part of the great lords that were prisoners. And always the prince served before the king as humbly as he could, and would not sit at the king's board for any desire that the king could make; but he said he was not sufficient to sit at the table with so great a prince as the king was. Then he said to the king, "Sir, for God's sake make no evil nor heavy cheer, though God this day did not consent to follow your will. For, sir, surely the king my father shall bear you as much honour and good will as he may do, and shall accord with you so reasonably that you shall ever be friends together after. And, sir, I think you ought to rejoice, though the day be not as you would have had it, for this day you have now the high renown of prowess, and have passed this day in valiantness all other of your party. Sir, I say this not to mock you, for all that be on our party, that saw every man's deeds, are plainly accorded by true sentence to give you the prize and chaplet."

Therewith the Frenchmen began to murmur, and said among themselves, how the prince had spoken nobly, and that by all estimation he should prove a noble man if God sent him life and to persevere in such good fortune.

1357.—How the prince conveyed the French king from Bordeaux into England.

Froissart, ch. 173. (1. § 403.)

Then he took the sea and certain lords of Gascony with him. The French king was in a vessel by himself to be more at his ease. There went with them two hundred men of arms and two thousand archers. For it was shewed the prince that the three estates, by whom the realm of France was governed, had laid in Normandy and Crotoy two great armies to the intent to meet with him, and to get the French king out of his hands if they might; but there were no such that appeared. And yet they were on the sea eleven days, and on the twelfth day they arrived at Sandwich. Then they issued out of their ships, and lay all that night and tarried there two days to refresh them, and on the third day they rode to Canterbury. When the king of England knew of their coming he commanded them of London to prepare themselves and their city to receive such a man as the French king was. Then they of London arrayed themselves by companies, and the chief masters' clothing different from the others. At Saint Thomas of Canterbury the French king and the prince made their offerings, and there tarried a day, and then rode to Rochester. And they tarried there that day, and the next day to Dartford, and the fourth day to London, where they were honourably received, and so they were in every good town as they passed. The French king rode through London on a white charger well-apparelled, and the prince on a little black hobby by him. Thus

he was conveyed along the city till he came to the
Savoy, the which house pertained to the heritage of
the Duke of Lancaster. There the French king kept
his house a long season, and thither came to see him
the king and the queen of England oftentimes, and
made him great feast and cheer. Anon after, by the
commandment of pope Innocent the Sixth, there
came into England the lord cardinal of Périgord
and the lord Nicholas, cardinal of Urgel. They
treated for a peace between the two kings, but they
could bring nothing to effect. But at last by good
means they procured a truce between the two kings
and all their allies, to endure till the feast of Saint
John the Baptist, in the year of our Lord God 1359.
And out of this truce was excepted the lord Philip of
Navarre and his allies, the countess of Montfort and
the duchy of Bretagny. Anon after the French king
was moved from the Savoy to the castle of Windsor,
and all his household. And went a-hunting and
a-hawking there about at his pleasure, and the lord
Philip, his son, with him. And all the other
prisoners abode still at London, and went to see
the king at their pleasure.

1360.—The treaty of Brétigny.

(The truce came to an end at the beginning of 1359, but the
Dauphin and the French estates would not accept the English
terms, and war was renewed. Edward gathered a larger army
than ever before, marched in November from Calais to Rheims,
which he failed to reduce, and then on towards Burgundy,
forcing its duke to purchase neutrality. Returning, he encamped

outside Paris, not venturing upon an assault; and at last, in
May, terms of peace were agreed upon.

Froissart, ch. 212 (1. § 474).

. . . "Our brother of France and his said son are
bound and promise to deliver and to leave to us, our
heirs and successors for ever, the counties, cities, towns,
castles, fortresses, lands, isles, rents, revenues and
other things as followeth, beside that we have and
hold already in Guienne and Gascony, to possess
perpetually by us and by our heirs and successors, all
that is in demesne and all that is in fee, by the time
and manner hereafter declared : that is to say, the
castle and county of Poitiers, and all the lands and
country of Poitou, with the fee of Thouars and the
lands of Belleville ; the city and castle of Saintes, and
all the lands and county of Saintonge, on both sides
the river of Charente, with the town and fortress of
Rochelle and their appurtenances; and the city and
castle of Agen and the country of Agenois; the city,
town, and castle of Perigord, and all the country
thereto belonging ; the city and castle of Limoges
and the land and country of Limousin ; the city
and castle of Cahors ; the castle and country of
Tarbes ; the lands, country, and county of Bigorre ;
the county, country, and land of Gaure ; the city and
castle of Angoulême and all the country thereto
pertaining; the city, town, and castle of Rodez,
and the county and country of Rouergne. And if
there be in the duchy of Guienne any lords, as the
earl of Foix, the earl of Armagnac, the earl of Lisle,
the viscount of Carmaine, the earl of Perigord, the

viscount of Limoges, or other, holding any lands within the foresaid bounds, they shall do homage to us and all other services due and accustomed. . . . Also the castle and town of Calais; the castle, town, and seignory of Merle; the towns, castles, and seignories of Sangates, Coulougne, Ham, Walles, and Oye; with the lands, woods, marshes, rivers, rents, revenues, seignories, advowsons of churches, and all other appurtenances and places. . . . .
. . . . . And it hath been agreed that our said brother and his eldest son should renounce all manner of sovereignty, resort, and rights, that he should have of any of them or for them; and that we should hold them as his neighbour, without any resort or sovereignty to our said brother or to the realm of France; and all the right that our said brother hath in the aforesaid things, he yieldeth and transferreth them to us perpetually. And also it is agreed that likewise we and our said son expressly renounce all things that ought not to be delivered to us by the said treaty, and specially of the name and right to the crown of France and to the realm and homage and sovereignty and domain of the duchy of Normandy, of the county of Touraine, and of the counties of Anjou and Maine, and the sovereignty and homage of the duchy of Brittany; except the right of the earl of Montfort, that he ought or might have in the duchy and county of Brittany, the which we reserve, and by express words put clean out of this our treaty, saving that we and our said brother when we come to Calais shall order that matter and settle a peace and concord between the earl Montfort and our cousin the lord Charles of Blois.

APPENDIX.

1. THE AUTHORITIES.

1. The greater number of the extracts in this book are taken from *Lord Berners' Translation of the Chronicle of Froissart.* Jehan Froissart was born at Valenciennes about 1337, and entered very early the service of his countrywoman Philippa of Hainault, the queen of Edward III. Upon her death in 1369 he returned to his native land, and it was then that, at the request of Philippa's brother-in-law, Robert of Namur, Froissart wrote the first version of his chronicle. The narrative of events before 1356 is based upon and, in the earlier part, verbally identical with the chronicle of Jehan le Bel, whose work is mentioned below; it is to this writer, and not to Froissart, that we are really indebted for some of the finest and best known passages, such as those describing the death-bed of Robert Bruce, and the siege of Calais. Froissart is never more than a chronicler; he is never a critical historian; and therefore, as was natural with his surroundings, this first version, which has alone become generally known, gives only the English version of the disputes between England and France and of the military operations. In reading his stirring narrative, this partiality for the English must never be forgotten.

Two manuscripts, those of Amiens and Valenciennes, give a later version of Book I. It seems to have been written about

1376, when Froissart was under the patronage of two firm adherents of France, Wenceslas of Brabant and Guy of Blois, and the ties binding him to England were all broken. This second narrative, in consequence, presents the French version of the events, differing frequently from the earlier account. And a still later version is preserved in one manuscript in Rome. Froissart had become a canon of Chimay, and is said to have died in 1410.

Froissart never attempts to examine evidence; his later versions are not improved and corrected editions of the earlier, but simply "other accounts." Each is but a well-written reproduction of the story told by the men around him; and, therefore, the editor has not scrupled to give the narrative as it is presented in the better known version, although it is somewhat partisan in character.

An additional reason for so doing is that he is thus enabled to make use of the vigorous sixteenth-century translation by *Lord Berners*, which reproduces the naive simplicity of the original far more than any modern translator could hope to do. John Bourchier, Lord Berners, who was born some sixty years after Froissart's death, it is said in 1467, served Henry VII. and Henry VIII. in war and diplomacy; and, after being for many years governor of Calais, died in that town in 1532. His translation of Froissart, undertaken at the command of Henry VIII., was printed by Pynson in black letter in 1523, and reprinted in 1812. The only changes that have been made are such verbal alterations as are necessary to make the sense clear. The references at the head of each extract are to the chapter in which it will be found in Berners, and, in brackets, to book and section in the only critical edition of Froissart that has appeared, that of M. Luce, for the Société de l'histoire de France.

2. Where the account is verbally or in the main derived from

Jehan le Bel, a reference is also given to the edition of that writer by M. Polain (1863). Of Jehan le Bel's personal history very little is known, save that he was of a patrician family of Liège, and was born about the end of the thirteenth century; that with his brother he accompanied John of Hainault to England, and took part in the expeditions against the Scots in the early years of Edward, so that the narrative is here that of an eyewitness; and that he became a canon of Liège, and died in 1370.

3. A great contrast to the detailed and picturesque narrative of Froissart is presented by *Adam of Murimuth*, who wrote short and simple annals of his own time from 1303 to 1346. He had unusual facilities for obtaining information, since he was employed in important diplomatic missions by Edward II. and Edward III., gaining as reward canonries at Hereford and London. His information, though very concise, is extremely valuable; an anonymous *Continuatio*, which is equally useful, carries on the narrative to 1380. His chronicle was edited by Mr. Hog for the English Historical Society in 1846.

4. Similar in character is the work of *Robert of Avesbury*, whose "History of the wonderful deeds of Edward III." has been only once printed, by Thomas Hearne in 1720. The writer describes himself as registrar of the archbishop's court at Canterbury. His work is more detailed than that of Murimuth or his continuator, and is equally trustworthy. Unfortunately it breaks off before the battle of Poitiers.

5. *Henry of Knighton*, a canon at Leicester, in the second half of the 15th century, had access to the papers of the earls of Leicester of the house of Lancaster, and follows with special interest and pride the actions of Henry of Derby, afterwards duke of Lancaster. He becomes independent in his narrative about the middle of the century; there is a break between 1367

and 1377; and then he continues his work to 1395. We owe to him many interesting notices of the social life of the time.

6. *The Chronicle of Lanercost*, the best authority for Border history and for the Scotch wars of the period, seems to have been given this name by mistake; it was more probably written by a Franciscan of the convent of Carlisle. The author gives full accounts of the campaigns and important battles, written with considerable vigour and rough humour; his sympathies are, of course, entirely English. The chronicle was edited by Mr. Stevenson for the Maitland and Bannatyne clubs in 1839.

7. Two interesting extracts have been made from a popular manual for confessors and the devout, called the *Ayenbite of Inwyt*, which has been edited by Mr. Morris. This is a translation made by Dan Michel, a Kentish monk, about 1340, of an earlier French treatise, and illustrates excellently the economic ideas of the time.

Besides these sources of information, use has been made of *Political Poems*, ed. Wright, the *Munimenta Gildhallae*, ed. Riley, the *Gesta Abbatum Monasterii S. Albani*, ed. Riley, all in the Rolls' Series; and of the two great collections, the *Statutes of the Realm*, and *Rymer's Fœdera* (ed. Record Commission). The illustrations of the *Skirmishing on the Tyne*, and of the battles of *Crecy* and *Poitiers* are from a 15th Century MS. of Froissart, preserved in the Paris *Bibliothèque Nationale* (MS. n. 2643).

192 APPENDIX.

2. THE ROYAL FAMILY.

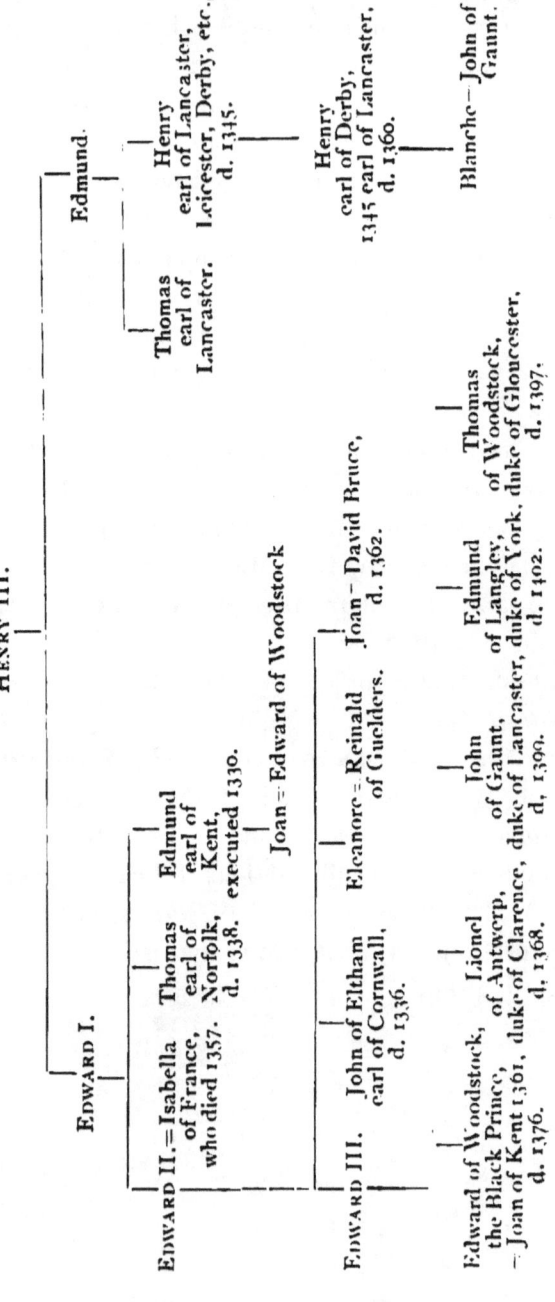

3. THE FRENCH SUCCESSION.

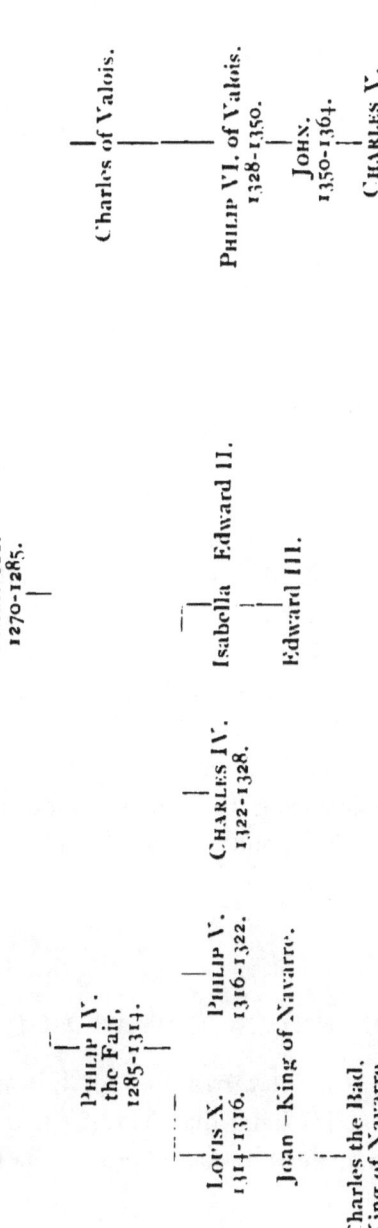

The three sons of Philip IV. having died without male heirs, Edward claimed the throne as the son of a daughter of Philip IV., against Philip of Valois, the son of a brother of Philip IV. But it had been long held that the succession to the French throne was regulated by what was called "the Salic law," which excluded females or their descendants. Edward declared that this only excluded females themselves (Joan of Navarre and the daughters of Philip IV's. sons), and that he had a better claim than their male children because he was born during the lifetime of the grandfather.

4. THE SUCCESSION TO BRITTANY.

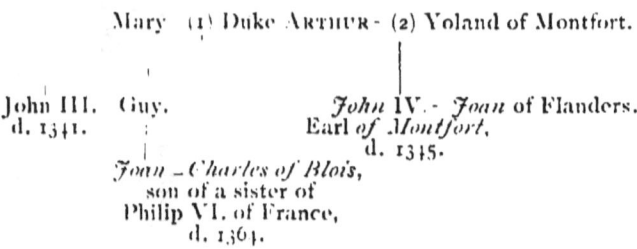

5. THE EMPEROR LEWIS IV. OF BAVARIA.

Lewis of Bavaria, who had been elected emperor in 1314, was engaged during the greater part of his life in a struggle with the popes, who were supported and prompted by the French kings. In 1324 pope John XXII. had put him under the ban and declared him deposed; in 1328 Lewis marched to Rome where he was crowned emperor, and set up an anti-pope. Edward seems to have thought it possible to make use of the imperial authority to obtain the support of all the princes of the Netherlands and of north-western Germany; but the campaign of 1340 proved that he could only expect assistance from them in proportion to the payments he could make them, and he soon dropped the title of vicar which had proved useless.

6. TAXATION UNDER EDWARD III.

By the *Confirmation of the Charters* in 1297 Edward I. had promised for himself and his heirs that henceforth they would not take "such manner of aids, tasks, or prises" as had been complained of, but "by the common assent of the realm," and that they would not take any tax on wool "without their common assent." But this left open to the king two ways of obtaining money without parliamentary sanction. There was first his right to *tallage* his demesne, (including most of the towns in the kingdom,) which belonged to him as landlord. Three instances of the exercise of this right are found after 1297, one in each of the reigns of Edward I., Edward II., and Edward III.; but by the statute of 1340 Edward III. was understood to give up the claim, and it was never afterwards put forward. The same statute was also explicit enough to deprive the king of another means of raising money which it had been urged did not violate the spirit of the Confirmation, namely by *voluntary grant of customs on the part of the merchants;* but it was necessary to expressly prohibit this practice in 1362, and again in 1371.

7. CHARLES OF NAVARRE.

Charles *the Bad* (a title which his cruelty early won for him) was the son of Joan the daughter of Louis X. of France. He succeeded in 1349 to the kingdom of Navarre and to the county of Evreux in Normandy; and in 1352 king John gave him his daughter in marriage. His power in Normandy, his great ability, and his claim to the French throne through his mother, made him so dangerous that John would have done well to make a close alliance with him; but instead of doing this, he refused to carry out certain promises which had been made to Joan of Navarre, and treated the young Charles with scant consideration. In revenge Charles caused the king's favourite, the constable,

Charles de la Cerda, to whom he attributed this illtreatment, to be assassinated in January 1354. Civil war was imminent; but, next month, John was induced to make terms with Charles and go through the ceremony of reconciliation. John wished only to gain time and began to gather troops. Charles, thereupon, made overtures to Edward and arranged to receive an English force at Cherbourg. Under the pressure of necessity John again in September accepted his conditions; and the English landing in Normandy was prevented at the last moment.

CONTENTS.

		PAGE
1327	Accession of Edward III.	5
	Charter to London	6
	Inroad of the Scots	8
	Campaign on the Tyne	9
	Murder of Edward II.	16
1328	Edward married to Philippa of Hainault	17
	Peace with Scotland	19
	Death of Robert Bruce	20
1328—9	Struggle between Mortimer and Lancaster	25
1330	Execution of Edmund of Kent	27
	Fall of Roger Mortimer	27
1331	Protection of Flemish weavers	29
1333	Battle of Halidon Hill	30
1334	Balliol does homage	33
	Oxford students at Stamford	34
1334—6	Expeditions into Scotland	35
1337	Export of wool prohibited	38
1329—1333	Robert of Artois	39
1337	Edward counselled to war against Philip	40
	Manifesto as to overtures rejected	43
	Jacques d'Artevelde	48
	Battle of Cadsand	52
1338	Defence of Dunbar	54
	Edward, vicar of the Empire	56
1339	Invasion of France	59
	Edward, "king of France"	63
	A college meeting	65
1340	A lesson on usury	68

CONTENTS.

		PAGE
	A lesson on trade	70
	Statute concerning taxation	71
	Battle of Sluys	73
	Siege of Tournay	77
1340—1	Removal of ministers	82
1341	Parliament	84
	A statute revoked	86
1342	The countess of Montfort in Hennebon	87
1344	Order of the garter	90
1345	Death of Artevelde	91
	Failure of the Bardi	95
1346	Edward crosses to Normandy	96
	Order of the English at Crecy	98
	Order of the French	100
	Battle of Crecy	102
	Battle of Neville's Cross	107
	Song of Neville's Cross	112
	Douglas at Tynemouth	115
1347	Surrender of Calais	116
1349	The Black Death	122
	Death of the abbot of St. Alban's	127
	The Flagellants	129
	Sir Amery of Pavia	130
1350	Edward at Calais	131
	Sir Eustace of Ribeaumont	134
	Naval battle with the Spaniards	136
1351	Coinage of groats and half-groats	137
	Statute of Provisors	138
1352	Statute of Treasons	140
1353	Statute of Præmunire	142
1354	The battle of the thirty	144
	Poem on the tourney of Ploërmel	149
1354	Lancaster at Avignon	155
	Troubles at Oxford	157
1355	The prince of Wales in Gascony	159
	Treachery of the king of Navarre	160
	Edward in Picardy	162
	The Scots capture Berwick	165

CONTENTS.

		PAGE
	Expedition of the prince of Wales ...	165
1356	Burnt Candlemas ...	167
	The night before Poitiers	168
	Order of the French	169
	The cardinal of Périgord	172
	The battle of Poitiers	174
	King John taken prisoner	179
	The prince entertains his captive	183
1357	John taken to England	184
1360	The treaty of Brétigny	185

APPENDIX.

1.	The Authorities...	188
2.	The royal family	192
3.	The French succession...	193
4.	The succession to Brittany	194
5.	The emperor Lewis IV. of Bavaria...	194
6.	Taxation under Edward III.	194
7.	Charles of Navarre	195

www.ingramcontent.com/pod-product-compliance
Lightning Source LLC
Chambersburg PA
CBHW020832230426
43666CB00007B/1193